LAW ESSENTIALS

Secured Transactions

Governing Law

3rd edition

This publication is designed to provide accurate and authoritative information regarding the subject matter covered. It is distributed with the understanding that the publisher, authors, or editors are not engaged in rendering legal or another professional service. If legal advice or other expert assistance is required, a competent professional's services should be sought.

Sterling Test Prep is not legally liable for mistakes, omissions, or inaccuracies in this publication's content. Sterling Test Prep does not guarantee that the user of this publication will pass the bar exam or achieve a performance level. Individual performance depends on many factors, including but not limited to the level of preparation, aptitude, and individual performance on test day.

3   2   1

ISBN-13: 979-8-8855700-7-7

Sterling Test Prep products are available at quantity discounts.

For more information, contact info@sterling–prep.com.

Sterling Test Prep
6 Liberty Square #11
Boston, MA 02109

©2022 Sterling Test Prep
Published by Sterling Test Prep
Printed in the U.S.A.

Customer Satisfaction Guarantee

Your feedback is important because we strive to provide the highest quality prep materials. Email us comments or suggestions.

info@sterling–prep.com

We reply to emails – check your spam folder

Thank you for choosing our book!

STERLING
Test Prep

Thousands of students use our study aids to prepare for law school exams and to pass the bar!

Passing the bar is essential for admission to practice law and launching your legal career.

This preparation guide describes the principles of substantive law governing the correct answers to exam questions. It was developed by legal professionals and law instructors who possess extensive credentials and have been admitted to practice law in several jurisdictions. The content is clearly presented and systematically organized for targeted preparation.

The performance on individual questions has been correlated with success or failure on the bar. By analyzing previously administered exams, the authors identified these predictive items and assembled the rules of law that govern the answers to questions tested. Learn the essential governing law to make fine-line distinctions among related principles and decide between tough choices on the exam. This knowledge is vital to excel in law school finals and pass the bar exam.

We look forward to being an essential part of your preparation and wish you great success in the legal profession!

Comprehensive Glossary of Legal Terms

Over 2,100 essential legal terms defined
and explained. An excellent reference
source for law students, practitioners and
readers seeking an understanding of legal
vocabulary and its application.

Landmark U.S. Supreme Court Cases: Essential Summaries

Learn important constitutional cases that
shaped American law. Understand how the
evolving needs of society intersect with the
U.S. Constitution. Short summaries of seminal
Supreme Court cases focused on issues and
holdings.

Visit our Amazon store

Table of Contents

SECURED TRANSACTIONS GOVERNING LAW (*continued*)

* *Abridged*

UNIFORM COMMERCIAL CODE (UCC) (*continued*)

UNIFORM COMMERCIAL CODE (UCC) (*continued*)

Validity of Security Agreements and Rights of Parties (*continued*)

UNIFORM COMMERCIAL CODE (UCC) (*continued*)

Perfection and Priority (*continued*)

UNIFORM COMMERCIAL CODE (UCC) (*continued*)

Perfection and Priority (*continued*)

UNIFORM COMMERCIAL CODE (UCC) (*continued*)

Perfection and Priority (*continued*)

UNIFORM COMMERCIAL CODE (UCC) (*continued*)

UNIFORM COMMERCIAL CODE (UCC) (*continued*)

UNIFORM COMMERCIAL CODE (UCC) (*continued*)

Default and Enforcement of Security Interest (*continued*)

UNIFORM COMMERCIAL CODE (UCC) (*continued*)

Default and Enforcement of Security Interest (*continued*)

UNIFORM COMMERCIAL CODE (UCC) (*continued*)

EXAM INFORMATION, PREP & TEST-TAKING STRATEGIES (*continued*)

EXAM INFORMATION, PREP & TEST-TAKING STRATEGIES *(continued)*

Secured Transactions
Governing Law

Secured Transactions is tested regularly as a standalone subject but may appear as a component of Contracts or Real Property. While specific items tested on Secured Transactions are somewhat predictable, they are challenging. The most tested items include classification of goods (e.g., consumer goods, inventory, equipment, farm products), security interest, attachment, perfection, and default. It is imperative to be familiar with the complex vocabulary.

For Secured Transaction questions, it is essential to understand the application of the Uniform Commercial Code Article 9. Per the National Conference of Bar Examiners (NCBE), assume that the Official Texts of Articles 1 and 9 of the UCC are adopted.

The Uniform Commercial Code (UCC) – Articles 1 and 9

History of the Uniform Commercial Code

The Uniform Law Commission (ULC), formed in 1892, promulgated uniform commercial laws.

The Uniform Negotiable Instruments Law, approved in 1896, was soon enacted in every state.

In 1940, the Uniform Law Commission drafted a comprehensive code to provide guidelines for commercial transactions.

In 1942, the ULC and the American Law Institute partnered to assemble the component commercial laws in a comprehensive Uniform Commercial Code (UCC) offered to the states for their consideration in 1951.

In 1953, Pennsylvania became the first state to adopt the UCC, and every other state had adopted the UCC within twenty years.

The UCC has been adopted, with some modifications, by every state and the District of Columbia, Guam, and the U.S. Virgin Islands.

UCC Article 1 – general provisions

Uniform Commercial Code (UCC) Article 1 contains definitions and general provisions applicable as default rules to transactions covered under other articles of the UCC.

Article 1 was revised in 2001, with a few minor amendments to harmonize with recent revisions of other UCC articles.

UCC Article 9 – Secured Transactions

The Uniform Commercial Code Article 9 provides a statutory framework that governs secured transactions, granting credit secured by personal property.

Each state maintains an office for filing financial statements to disclose security interests in encumbered property publicly.

A substantial revision to Article 9 was completed in 1998 and adopted in all states.

Secured transactions and UCC law

The law in the U.S. covers the creation and enforcement of a security interest.

A secured transaction happens when a person or business borrows money to acquire property, including real estate, vehicles, or business equipment.

A security interest exists when a borrower enters a contract that allows the lender (secured party) to take collateral the borrower owns if the borrower cannot repay the loan.

The term *security interest* is often used interchangeably with *lien* in the U.S.

Purpose of secured transactions

A security interest promotes economic security because it provides the lender with the promise of repayment. If the borrower defaults on the loan, the lender should recoup the loan amount by taking the agreed-upon asset used as collateral and selling it.

A security interest is particularly valuable in bankruptcy because secured creditors collect debts before creditors without a security interest.

Law governs secured transactions

A security interest generally is created with a security agreement, which is a contract governed by UCC Article 9 and state laws governing contracts.

Article 9 of the UCC governs voluntary and commercial transaction and creates an interest in personal property.

Real property secured transactions, such as for a real estate mortgage, are not governed by Article 9 but by real property laws that vary among states.

Fixtures include personal property attached to real property (e.g., furnace, kitchen cabinets).

Statutory liens arise from laws providing a right to retain property against its owner as security for obligations, governed by enabling statutes.

Creating security interests under Article 9

For a security interest to be enforceable against the debtor and third parties, value must be exchanged for the collateral.

UCC Article 9 sets forth three requirements:

1) the debtor must have rights in the collateral or the ability to convey rights in the collateral to a secured party, and either

2) the debtor must have "authenticated" a security agreement describing the collateral, or

3) the creditor must be in possession of the collateral.

When Article 9 requirements are satisfied, the security interest "attaches" to the collateral and becomes enforceable.

Usually, a borrower and lender sign a security agreement.

Such a security agreement usually includes:

1) a description of the borrower's collateral,

2) a description of the obligation it secures,

3) an identification of what constitutes a default,

4) rights of the creditor if the borrower defaults,

5) requirements of the debtor for the care of and insurance maintained on the collateral, and

6) other obligations of the parties to the transaction.

A statute of frauds within UCC Article 9 requires the security agreement be in writing.

An exception to this requirement be in writing is when a security interest is pledged.

A pledge is when a borrower gives the collateral to the lender in exchange for a loan (e.g., goods to a pawnbroker in exchange for a cash loan).

If a security agreement does not exist, and the security interest is not pledged, but the transaction appears to be an Article 9 transaction, the court may recognize it as such by applying the composite document rule.

The court will consider documents supporting the security agreement and create an enforceable security interest by reading the documents.

The parties must authenticate the documents specified by this rule; if this proves impossible, the security agreement fails.

Perfection

The perfection of a security agreement allows a secured party to prioritize the collateral over a third party, should the borrower default on the loan.

Perfection becomes important if other creditors have an interest in the secured property because a secured creditor's obligation will be satisfied before other liens; known as priority.

The creditor with the highest priority will be repaid before others if the borrower defaults and foreclosure occurs.

Three exceptions exist for filing for perfection:

> automatic redemption,
>
> possession, and
>
> taking control of a deposit account.

The typical way to perfect a security interest is by filing a notice in a public office.

The filing of a public notice puts other creditors on notice of the attached security interest in the creditor's property.

The required filing most frequently is a financing statement.

For a financing statement to be valid, it must include:

> 1) the debtor's name,
>
> 2) the secured party's name or representative, and
>
> 3) a description of the property covered by the statement.

If any of the three elements are missing from a financing statement, the security interest will not be perfected.

A financing statement is valid for five years from the date it was filed and can be extended.

The United States does not have a central place for filing.

Each state has a UCC filing system; though the filing office varies from state to state, most commonly, it is the Secretary of State's office.

For the most part, each county in the U.S. has a real estate recording office where Article 9 fixture filings can be done.

Article 9 – Secured Transactions

Introduction to secured transactions

Article 9 addresses issues about the priority of parties concerning the collateral.

Issues concerning the foreclosure method of a security interest, the rights of the debtor when the secured party wants to foreclose the security interest, the rights of parties in bankruptcy, or the intricacies of exotic types of security interests have not been asked and will not be discussed.

An approach to priority problems

For Article 9, questions about the rights of the parties resolve the following issues.

1) Is the security interest of each claimant and other secured parties valid?

2) Have the various security interests attached? When did attachment occur?

3) Is the collateral consumer goods, business equipment, or business inventory?

4) Are any of the security interests purchase money security interests?

5) Has each security interest been perfected, and when was each perfected?

6) Has the property been acquired from the debtor by a good faith purchaser?

7) What priority rule applies to the claims of each party?

Creating the security interest by security agreement

A security agreement establishes a security interest.

A security agreement must be in writing and contain a statement that a security interest in collateral, described in the agreement, is created, and the debtor must sign it.

A security agreement can agree to give a security interest in property that the debtor will acquire in the future. Such an interest does not attach until the debtor obtains an interest in the property.

Creating the security interest by pledge

A pledge occurs when the secured party takes possession of the debtor's property with an oral or written agreement that the secured party will hold the property to secure a debt.

Notes for active learning

Attaching the Security Interest

Collateral for the security interest

Even if there is a security agreement or a pledge, a creditor has no security interest in a piece of collateral until that interest attaches to the collateral.

If a security interest has been properly created, the debtor must receive value, which is defined as consideration to support a contract.

Examples of "value" are:

1) a binding agreement by the secured party to extend credit, or

2) total or partial satisfaction of a pre-existing claim, or

3) the debtor's acceptance of delivery of the collateral per the pre-existing contract.

Debtor must have rights in the collateral

This issue does not arise if the debtor is the collateral owner.

The debtor may not yet acquire title to the collateral because:

1) it is being manufactured according to a purchase order,

2) the security interest would not arise until the goods are identified in the contract.

Identified goods during seller's insolvency

The buyer has a particular property interest in the goods, which entitles them to obtain identified goods (for which they made at least partial payment) upon the seller's insolvency.

This interest gives certain rights to:

1) specific performance, and

2) an insurable interest in the identified goods.

Notes for active learning

Collateral

Types of collateral

Bar exam questions under Article 9 rarely deal with sophisticated business arrangements in collateral, such as accounts receivable.

Bar exam questions generally deal with tangible personal property.

There are four important categories for a priority problem:

1)　consumer goods,

2)　machinery used in business (different rules for perfection),

3)　business inventory,

4)　collateral, which is attached to real estate, is a fixture.

Mortgagee *vs.* secured party

The rules for filing to perfect a security interest in such collateral against the owner and mortgagees of the real property are different from that of property not so affixed.

Special priority rules apply for mortgagees of real property.

The term *fixtures* is defined by law.

In most states, whether a chattel has become a fixture depends on the objective intent of the owner of the property.

Where the chattel is so affixed to the realty that its identity is lost, or where it cannot be removed without material injury to the realty itself, any security interest in the property as personalty is lost, and the owner of the real estate is the owner of the collateral.

If the property can be removed from the real estate without substantial damage, the secured party can preserve their security interest in the collateral with proper filing.

A fixture filing must be made to obtain priority over subsequent interests in real estate.

Notes for active learning

Perfected Security Interests

Notice by perfection

The perfection of a security interest is similar to the process of recording a mortgage.

Its purpose is to give notice to the world that the secured party has a security interest in specified collateral of the debtor to let other potential creditors know that the secured party has a claim on that collateral to satisfy its debt.

If a secured party fails to perfect its security interest, it risks losing its ability to exercise a secured party's rights in the collateral.

Perfection of a security interest established by pledge

Possession of the collateral by the secured party is sufficient to perfect a pledge.

No filing is required.

Perfection by filing

A security interest is protected by filing only if accomplished as prescribed by Article 9 and filed in the proper place.

Except where the Code provides a grace period, perfection occurs at the time of filing or when the property attaches, whichever is later.

Automatic perfection

An interest in consumer goods is automatically perfected as soon as the secured party's security interest attaches without filing or possession.

Certificates of title for motor vehicles – perfection

When a car is registered, a "certificate of title" is issued.

When dealing with the motor vehicle, the certificate of title determines who owns the car and the extent to which the named owner's title is subject to others' interests.

A security interest in an automobile used as consumer goods or equipment is perfected only by applying for a certificate of title, showing the security interest on it.

There is a ten-day grace period for perfecting a security interest on a motor vehicle that operates in the same manner as the grace period for a purchase money security interest.

Filing of a security interest

The primary object of the filing is to give interested parties notice of the security interest.

The filing requirement is satisfied if a security agreement or financing statement containing the following information is filed:

1) Name and address of the debtor and secured party.

2) Description of the collateral by items or types; must reasonably identify what is described.

3) Signature of only the debtor.

Minor errors will not affect the validity of the filing.

Amendments are permitted.

The proper place of filing a security interest is with the Secretary of State's office.

Characterizing the Status of Contesting Third Parties

Third-party claims to the collateral

Before applying the rules of priority, characterize the various parties' status.

In most questions, the parties fall into four groups:

1) general creditors of the debtor,

2) other secured creditors of the debtor,

3) creditors who have obtained a judicial lien against the debtor's property, and

4) transferees of the title to the property.

In general, to assert their rights, each of the types of parties must have no actual knowledge of another party's security interest when they gave credit or purchased the property.

The exception to this rule is the buyer in the ordinary course of business who takes free of a lien even if they knew about it.

General creditors

A *general creditor* has a claim (including a judgment) against the debtor but no lien against the property in question.

A secured party always prevails over a general creditor.

Lien creditors

A general creditor who obtains a pre-judgment or post-judgment lien of the property in issue is a lien creditor.

An assignee for the benefit of creditors and a trustee in bankruptcy is a lien creditor.

Their priority position for collateral is determined by the time they obtained the lien.

Other secured parties

Secured parties have security interests created under Article 9.

Rules for the priorities of secured parties are established by Article 9.

Transferees

Transferees have acquired the debtor's ownership in the collateral instead of persons with lesser interests, such as secured parties.

Buyer in the ordinary course of business

The Buyer in Ordinary Course of Business is the most important and favored party in the Commercial Code.

Section 1-201 defines the buyer in the ordinary course of business as:

> A person, who in good faith and without knowledge that the sale violates the ownership rights or security interests of a third party in the goods, buys in the ordinary course from a person in the business of selling goods of that kind but omits a pawnbroker.

"Buying" may be for cash or by an exchange of other property or on secured or unsecured credit and includes receiving goods or title under a pre-existing contract for sale.

This does not include a transfer in bulk or as security for the satisfaction of a money debt.

To disqualify the buyer, there must be knowledge not merely of the third party's interests but that the sale violates those interests.

Buyers of appliances, automobiles or other inventory from retailers are usually buyers in the ordinary course of business.

A retailer buying inventory from a wholesaler is a buyer in the ordinary course of business.

Owners of real estate to which the collateral is attached

Owners of real estate to which the collateral is attached, and their mortgagees, may have rights in the collateral if it can be characterized as real estate if the perfection of the security interest did not include a filing in the registry of deeds.

Priority Rules

Preparation to apply the priority rules

When presented with a priority problem, the first step is to take each party and apply the governing law to determine their status.

If the party is claiming rights as a secured party, determine if they have a valid security interest in the property, when and if attached, when was it perfected.

Check if the secured party has a purchase money security interest.

Check if the secured party knew a prior unperfected security interest when they perfected their interest.

If the title has been transferred from the person who initially granted the security interest, determine if the transferee was a *bona fide* purchaser.

Once these characterizations are completed, apply the following rules to determine priority.

Secured party *vs.* unsecured creditor

If the secured party has a valid security interest in the collateral, they prevail over an unsecured creditor, even if the secured party does not perfect.

Secured party *vs.* statutory lien creditor

Artisans who perform work on personal property (car repairman) have a lien on the property for the work performed if they retain possession.

That lien is superior to a secured party's lien, perfected before the statutory lien arose.

Secured party *vs.* lien creditor

A general creditor can become a lien creditor by suing the debtor and establishing a lien on the debtor's property.

That lien becomes equivalent to a perfected security interest when the creditor has a lien on the goods.

To determine whose lien has priority, compare the date of the secured party's interest with when the judicial lien was perfected.

A judicial lien is perfected when the sheriff takes possession.

The first party to achieve the perfected lien status prevails.

Notes for active learning

Purchase Money Secured Interest (PMSI)

Priority rules for a purchase money security interest

Purchase money security interests (PMSI) have special rules of priority.

A purchase money security interest arises if the security interest is in favor of:

>   1) seller of the collateral to secure all or part of its price; or

>   2) a person who, by making advances or incurring an obligation, gives value to enable the debtor to acquire rights in or the use of collateral if such value is so used.

"Grace period" for purchase money security interests

Where the security interest is a purchase money security interest, there is a ten-day grace period for filing the notice of a security interest.

If the interest is filed within ten days of the date the debtor comes into possession of the collateral, the filing reverts to the time the debtor took possession.

This reversion is good against only bulk transferees and lien creditors.

It does not apply to good faith purchasers.

Except for collateral in the form of inventory, a purchase money security interest prevails over other security interests, provided it is perfected within ten days of the time possession is given to the debtor.

First in time, first in right

Where there are two or more secured parties contesting rights in the same collateral, the basic rule is again first in time, first in right.

There are three rules to determine who is first in time.

>   1) If both security interests are perfected, the first to perfect by properly filing prevails.
>
>   If a security agreement includes after-acquired property, no security interest in that property arises until the interest attaches when the debtor obtains possession.
>
>   Filing, not attachment, determines priority.
>
>   A creditor who obtained a security interest in the after-acquired property and perfected it by filing prevails over a non-purchase money security interest filed later.

2) If one security interest is perfected and the other not, the perfected security interest prevails.

3) If neither security interest is perfected, the person whose interest first attached will prevail, but since neither party has completed the filing necessary for perfection, either party can perfect first and prevail.

PMSI *vs.* non-PMSI – who perfected first

Where the collateral is anything other than inventory (e.g., machinery), the purchase money secured interest (PMSI) party prevails over other security interests in the collateral.

This includes against those who hold a security interest in after-acquired collateral and have previously perfected if the purchase money secured interest party perfects within 10 days after the debtor obtains possession.

If the purchase-money collateral is inventory, the purchase money security holder will not prevail against a previously perfected security interest in that inventory unless the party claiming under the purchase money security interest:

1) perfects before giving possession to the debtor, and

2) gives notice to other secured parties of record.

Secured Party *vs.* Transferees of the Collateral

General rule

A purchaser of the collateral who gives value and takes delivery without knowledge of an outstanding unperfected security interest prevails over the secured party.

This rule applies to a purchase money security interest sold during the ten-day grace period.

A person who purchases collateral where there is a perfected security interest owns the property subject to the security interest unless one of the following special rules applies:

Where a debtor has permission to sell the collateral

If the secured party gives the debtor permission to sell the collateral, the secured party's security interest is extinguished upon sale; the buyer and subsequent purchasers take free and clear and with the security interest.

For example, if the bank has a perfected lien on all refrigerators in the dealer's stock and gives the dealer the right to sell them free of the collateral, the buyer will prevail even if they knew of the lien and was not a purchaser in the ordinary course of the seller's business.

Consumer buyers

Consumer buyers take free and clear of unfiled security interests.

For example, a buyer gives the seller a purchase money security interest on a refrigerator they purchase as consumer goods. Seller does not file the security interest, but it is perfected under the rule of automatic perfection without filing for consumer goods. If the buyer later sells that refrigerator to another consumer, that consumer takes free of the perfected security interest.

Notes for active learning

Bona Fide Purchasers in Ordinary Course of Business

A buyer in the ordinary course of business buys from a seller of goods of that kind, in good faith and without knowledge that the sale violates others' interests.

The buyer takes free of other interests, even the interest of an owner of the property who merely deposited the property with the seller.

A buyer in the ordinary course takes free of security interests created by the seller, even though the security interests are filed or otherwise perfected even though the buyer in the ordinary course knew of the security interest.

Secured Party *vs.* Landlord of the Debtor

The secured party has the right to remove personal property, which has become a fixture, and sell it if they had perfected that interest by filing it following the ordinary filing rules and has also filed it in the registry of deeds where the land lies.

The secured party's rights in the collateral are superior to the landlord and the landlord's mortgage, even if the mortgage was filed before the security interest.

If the collateral is so entwined with the real estate that it is not possible to remove it without significant damage to the real estate, the landlord prevails.

Relationship matrix

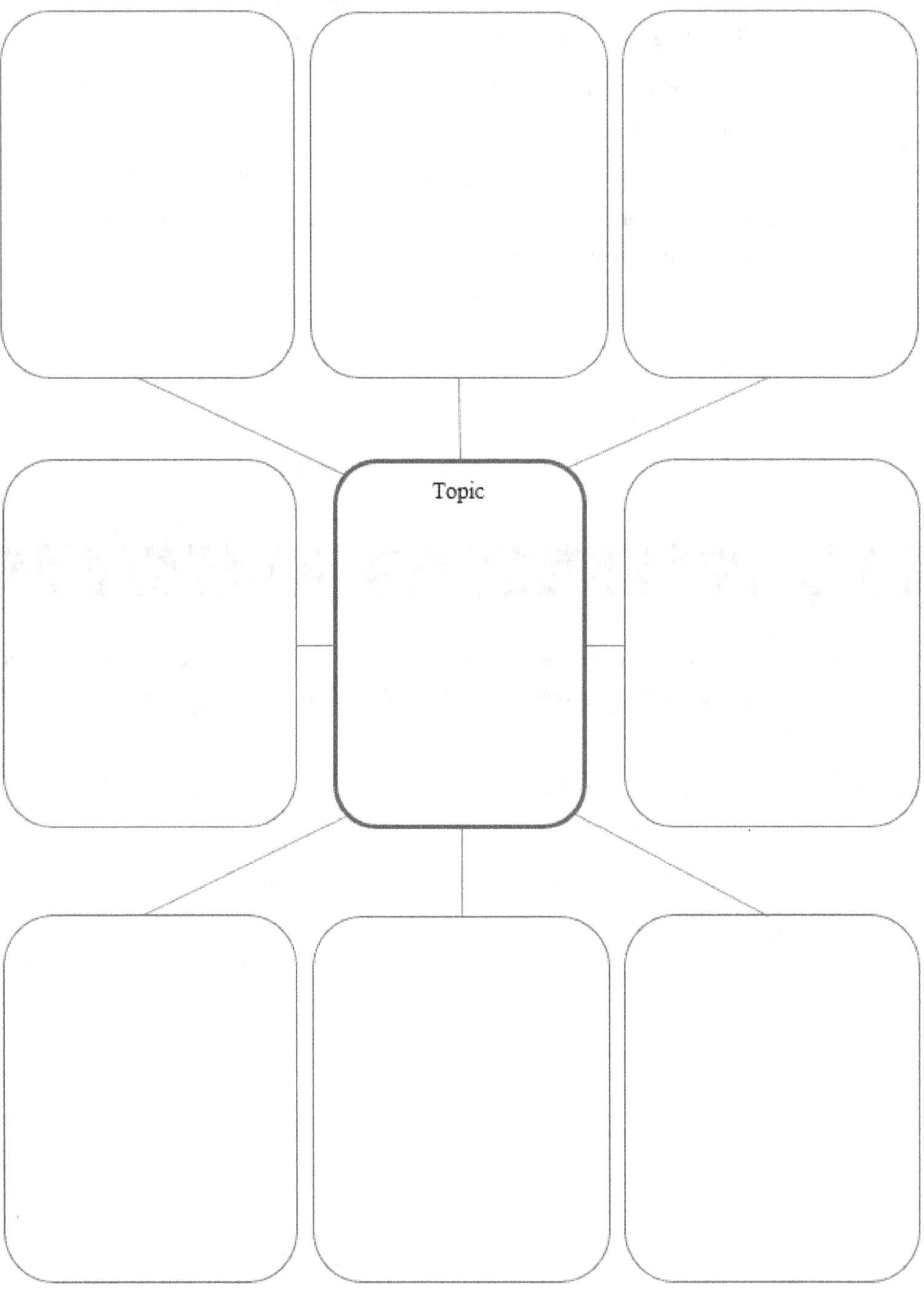

Notes for active learning

Notes for active learning

Review Questions

Multiple-choice questions

1. In a credit transaction, the creditor will usually take a security interest through:

    I. The mortgage note

    II. Collateral

    III. A high-interest rate

A. I only   **C.** II and III only

B. II only   **D.** I, II and III

2. A loans B money, and C promises to pay the loan if B defaults. C is a:

A. Surety   **C.** Cosigner

B. Guarantor   **D.** Assignee

3. Judgment-proof means that the creditor:

A. Will likely be able to collect   **C.** May not collect

B. Has won many lawsuits   **D.** Is a good litigator

4. To be a valid written security agreement, it must:

    I. Identify the collateral

    II. Contain the debtor's promise to repay the creditor

    III. Set forth the creditor's rights upon default

A. I only   **C.** III only

B. II only   **D.** I, II and III

5. In a guaranty arrangement, who agrees to pay the debt of the principal debtor?

    I. The principal debtor

    II. The guarantor

    III. The codebtor

A. I only   **C.** II only

B. I and II only   **D.** II and III only

6. Contractors that provide time and materials are protected in their investments through:

    I. Mechanic's lien
    II. Tax lien
    III. Testamentary lien

A. I only

B. I and II only

C. I and III only

D. I, II and III

True/false questions

7. Security means collateral.

    True   False

8. In a credit transaction, the borrower is the debtor, and the lender is the creditor.

    True   False

9. If a mortgage is not recorded, the creditor is still protected, at least as it concerns the debtor's obligation to pay.

    True   False

10. Unsecured credit requires collateral.

    True   False

11. Article 2 of the UCC governs secured transactions in personal property.

    True   False

12. A mortgage is a three-party instrument.

    True   False

13. Financing statements, having been filed, perfect the creditor's security interest.

    True   False

14. A Visa card is an example of unsecured credit.

    True   False

15. A financing statement is required if the creditor has physical possession of collateral.

    True   False

16. The mortgagee is the home buyer, and the mortgagor is the bank.

    True   False

17. In a surety arrangement, a third-person promises to be liable for paying another's debt.

    True   False

18. The owner-debtor is the mortgagee.

    True   False

Answer keys

1: B

2: B

3: C

4: D

5: C

6: A

7: True	16: False
8: True	17: True
9: True	18: False
10: False	
11: False	
12: False	
13: True	
14: True	
15: False	

UNIFORM COMMERCIAL CODE (UCC)

Annotated Sections

STERLING
Test Prep

General Provisions of the Uniform Commercial Code

The following chapters are for reference.

The National Conference of Bar Examiners (NCBE) listed chapters for Article 1 and Article 9 (Secured Transactions) are included below.

§ 1-103. Construction of the UCC Promotes Purposes and Policies

The Uniform Commercial Code must be liberally construed and applied to promote its underlying purposes and policies, which are:

a) to clarify and modernize the law governing commercial transactions;

b) to permit the continued expansion of commercial practices through custom, usage, and agreement of the parties; and

c) to make uniform the law among the various jurisdictions.

Unless displaced by the provisions of the Uniform Commercial Code, the principles of law and equity, including the law merchant and the law relative to capacity to contract, principal and agent, estoppel, fraud, misrepresentation, duress, coercion, mistake, bankruptcy, and other validating or invalidating cause supplement its provisions.

§ 1-105. Severability

If any provision or clause of the Uniform Commercial Code or its application is held invalid, the invalidity does not affect other provisions or applications of the UCC, which can be given effect without the invalid provision or application, and to this end, the provisions of the UCC are severable.

§ 1-108. Electronic Signatures in Commerce Act

This article modifies and supersedes the federal Electronic Signatures in Global and National Commerce Act, 15 U.S.C. Section 7001 *et seq.*, except that nothing in this article modifies or supersedes that Act or authorizes electronic delivery of any of the notices described in that Act.

General Definitions and Principles of Interpretation

§ 1-201. General Definitions

Subject to definitions in other articles of the UCC that apply to articles or parts thereof:

Action, as a judicial proceeding, includes recoupment, counterclaim, set-off, suit in equity, and other proceeding in which rights are determined.

Aggrieved party means a party entitled to pursue a remedy.

Agreement means the bargain of the parties as found in their language or inferred from other circumstances, including course of performance, course of dealing, or usage of trade.

Bearer means a person in possession of a negotiable instrument, the document of title, or certificated security payable to the bearer or endorsed in blank.

Bill of lading means a document evidencing the receipt of goods for shipment issued by a person engaged in the business of transporting or forwarding goods.

Buyer in the ordinary course of business means a person that buys goods in good faith, without knowledge that the sale violates the rights of another in the goods, and in the ordinary course from a person, other than a pawnbroker, in the business of selling goods of that kind.

A person buys goods in the ordinary course if the sale to the person comports with the usual or customary practices in the business in which the seller is engaged or with the seller's own usual or customary practices.

A buyer in the ordinary course of business may buy for cash by exchanging other property or on secured or unsecured credit and may acquire goods or documents of title under a preexisting contract for sale.

Only a buyer that takes possession of the goods or has a right to recover the goods from the seller under Article 2 may be a buyer in the ordinary course of business.

Buyer in the ordinary course of business does not include a person that acquires goods in a transfer in bulk or as security for or in total or partial satisfaction of a money debt.

Contract means the total legal obligation resulting from the parties' agreement as determined by the Uniform Commercial Code as supplemented by any other applicable laws.

Creditor includes a general creditor, a secured creditor, a lien creditor, and any representative of creditors, including an assignee for the benefit of creditors, a trustee in bankruptcy, a receiver in equity, and an executor or administrator of an insolvent debtor.

Delivery, for an instrument, a document of title, or chattel paper, means voluntary transfer of possession.

Document of title includes bill of lading, dock warrant, dock receipt, warehouse receipt or order for the delivery of goods, and other document which in the regular course of business is treated as adequately evidencing that the person in possession of it is entitled to receive and dispose of the document and the goods it covers.

A document of the title must purport to be issued by or addressed to a bailee and purport to cover goods in the bailee's possession identified or fungible portions of an identified mass.

Fault means a default, breach, or wrongful act or omission.

Fungible good means: 1) goods of which any unit, by nature or usage of trade, is the equivalent of any other like unit; or 2) goods that by agreement are treated as equivalent.

Good faith means honesty and the observance of reasonable commercial standards of fair dealing.

Holder means 1) the person in possession of a negotiable instrument that is payable to the bearer or an identified person in possession, or 2) the person in possession of a document of title if the goods are deliverable to bearer or the order of the person in possession.

Insolvency proceeding includes an assignment for the benefit of creditors or proceedings intended to liquidate or rehabilitate the estate of the person involved.

Insolvent means:

> 1) having ceased to pay debts in the ordinary course of business other than as a result of *bona fide* dispute;
>
> 2) being unable to pay debts as they become due; or
>
> 3) being insolvent within the meaning of federal bankruptcy law.

Party (distinguished from "third party") means a person engaged in a transaction or agreed subject to the Uniform Commercial Code.

Present value means the amount as of a date certain of one or more sums payable in the future, discounted to the date certain by use of either an interest rate specified by the parties if that rate is not manifestly unreasonable at the time the transaction is entered into or, if an interest rate is not so specified, a commercially reasonable rate that considers the facts at the time the transaction is entered into.

Purchase means taking by sale, lease, mortgage, pledge, lien, security interest, issue or reissue, gift, or other voluntary transaction creating an interest in the property.

Record means information that is inscribed on a tangible medium or that is stored in an electronic or other medium and is retrievable in perceivable form.

Remedy means any remedial right to which an aggrieved party is entitled with or without resort to a tribunal.

Security interest means an interest in personal property or fixtures which secures payment or performance of an obligation.

Security interest includes any interest of a consignor and a buyer of accounts, chattel paper, a payment intangible, or a promissory note in a transaction subject to Article 9.

A seller or lessor may acquire a security interest by complying with Article 9.

Surety includes a guarantor or other secondary obligor.

Unauthorized signature means a signature made without actual, implied, or apparent authority. The term includes a forgery.

Warehouse receipt means a receipt issued by a person engaged in the business of storing goods for hire.

§ 1-202. Notice; Knowledge

A person has **notice** of a fact if the person:

> 1) has actual knowledge of it;
>
> 2) has received a notice or notification of it; or
>
> 3) from the facts and circumstances known to the person at the time in question, has reason to know that it exists.

Knowledge means actual knowledge. "Knows" has a corresponding meaning.

Discover, or **learn**, refer to knowledge rather than to reason to know.

A person **notifies** or **gives** a notice or notification to another person by taking such steps as may be reasonably required to inform the other person in the ordinary course, whether the other person comes to know of it.

A person **receives** a notice or notification when:

> 1) it comes to that person's attention; or
>
> 2) it is duly delivered in a form reasonable under the circumstances at the place of business through which the contract was made or at another location held out by that person as the place for receipt of such communications.

Notice or knowledge received by an organization is effective for a particular transaction from the time it is brought to the attention of the individual conducting that transaction or should have been brought to the individual's attention if the organization had exercised due diligence.

An organization exercises due diligence if it maintains reasonable routines for communicating significant information to the person conducting the transaction, and there is reasonable compliance with the routines.

Due diligence does not require an individual acting for the organization to communicate information unless the communication is part of the individual's regular duties or the individual has reason to know of the transaction and that the transaction would be materially affected by the information.

§ 1-203. Lease Distinguished from Security Interest

A transaction in the form of a lease creates a security interest if the consideration that the lessee is to pay the lessor for the right to possession and use of the goods is an obligation for the term of the lease and is not subject to termination by the lessee, and:

1) the original term of the lease is equal to or greater than the remaining economic life of the goods;

2) the lessee is bound to renew the lease for the remaining economic life of the goods or is bound to become the owner of the goods;

3) the lessee has an option to renew the lease for the remaining economic life of the goods for no additional consideration or nominal additional consideration upon compliance with the lease agreement; or

4) the lessee has an option to become the owner of the goods for no additional consideration or nominal additional consideration upon compliance with the lease agreement.

A lease transaction does *not* create a security interest merely because:

1) the present value of the consideration the lessee is obligated to pay the lessor for the right to possession and use of the goods is substantially equal to or is greater than the fair market value of the goods at the time the lease is entered into;

2) the lessee assumes the risk of loss of the goods;

3) the lessee agrees to pay, for the goods, taxes, insurance, filing, recording, or registration fees, or service or maintenance costs;

4) the lessee has an option to renew the lease or to become the owner of the goods;

5) the lessee has an option to renew the lease for a fixed rent that is equal to or greater than the reasonably predictable fair market rent for the use of the goods for the term of the renewal at the time the option is to be performed; or

6) the lessee has an option to become the owner of the goods for a fixed price that is equal to or greater than the predictable fair market value of the goods at the time the option is to be performed.

Additional consideration is nominal if it is less than the lessee's reasonably predictable cost of performing under the lease agreement if the option is not exercised.

Additional consideration is *not nominal* if:

>1) when the option to renew the lease is granted to the lessee, the rent is stated to be the fair market rent for the use of the goods for the term of the renewal determined at the time the option is to be performed; or

>2) when the option to become the owner of the goods is granted to the lessee, the price is stated to be the fair market value of the goods determined at the time the option is to be performed.

The "remaining economic life of the goods" and "reasonably predictable" fair market rent, fair market value, or cost of performing under the lease agreement must be determined regarding the facts and circumstances at the time the transaction is entered.

§ 1-303. Course of Performance, Course of Dealing, and Usage of Trade

A course of performance is a sequence of conduct between the parties to a particular transaction that exists if:

>1) the agreement of the parties for the transaction involves repeated occasions for performance by a party; and

>2) the other party, with knowledge of the nature of the performance and opportunity for objection to it, accepts the performance or acquiesces in it without objection.

A **course of dealing** is a sequence of conduct concerning previous transactions between the parties to a particular transaction that is regarded as establishing a common basis of understanding for interpreting their expressions.

A **usage of trade** is any practice or method of dealing having such regularity in a place, vocation, or trade for an expectation that it will be observed for the transaction in question.

If it is established that such a usage is embodied in a trade code or similar record, the interpretation of the record is a question of law.

A **course of performance** or **course of dealing** between the parties or **usage of trade** in the vocation or trade in which they are engaged or of which they are or should be aware is relevant in ascertaining the meaning of the parties' agreement, may give meaning to specific terms of the agreement, and may supplement or qualify the terms of the agreement.

A usage of trade applicable in the place in which part of the performance under the agreement is to occur may be so utilized as to that part of the performance.

The express terms of an agreement and applicable course of performance, course of dealing, or usage of trade must be construed whenever reasonable as consistent with each other.

If such a construction is unreasonable:

1) express terms prevail over course of performance, course of dealing, and usage of trade;

2) course of performance prevails throughout dealing and usage of trade; and

3) course of dealing prevails over usage of trade.

A course of performance is relevant to show a waiver or modification of any term inconsistent with the course of performance.

Evidence of a relevant usage of trade offered by one party is not admissible unless that party has given the other party notice to prevent unfair surprise to the other party.

§ 1-304. Obligation of Good Faith

Duties within the UCC impose an obligation of *good faith* in performance and enforcement.

§ 1-305. Remedies to be Liberally Administered

The remedies provided by the UCC must be liberally administered so the aggrieved party may be put in as good a position as if the other party had entirely performed.

Consequential, special damages or penal damages do not apply except as expressly provided in the UCC or by another rule of law.

Any right or obligation declared by the UCC is enforceable by action unless the provision declaring it specifies a different and limited effect.

§ 1-307. Prima Facie Evidence by Third-Party Documents

A document in due form purporting to be a bill of lading, certificate of insurance, inspector's certificate, or other document authorized by the contract to be issued by a third party is prima facie evidence of its authenticity and the facts stated in the document by the third party.

§ 1-308. Performance or Acceptance Under Reservation of Rights

A party with explicit reservation of rights performs or promises performance or assents to performance in a manner demanded by the other party does not prejudice the rights reserved; it does not apply to an accord and satisfaction.

Such words as **without prejudice**, **under protest**, or the like are sufficient.

§ 1-309. Option to Accelerate at-Will

A term providing that one party may accelerate payment or performance or additional collateral "at-will" or when the party "deems itself insecure" means that the party has the power to do so only if that party in good faith believes that the prospect of payment or performance is impaired.

The burden of establishing a lack of good faith is on the party against which the power has been exercised.

§ 1-310. Subordinated Obligations

An obligation may be issued as subordinated to the performance of another obligation of the person obligated, or a creditor may subordinate its right to performance of an obligation by agreement with either the person obligated, or another creditor of the person obligated.

Subordination does not create a security interest as against either the common debtor or a subordinated creditor.

Article 9 – Secured Transactions

§ 9-102. Definitions

Accession means goods physically united with other goods such that the identity of the original goods is not lost.

Account means a right to payment of a monetary obligation, whether or not earned by performance, (i) for property that has been or is to be sold, leased, licensed, assigned, or disposed of, (ii) for services rendered, (iii) for a policy of insurance issued, (iv) for a secondary obligation incurred, (v) for energy provided, (vi) for the use of a vessel under a contract, (vii) arising out of the use of a credit card, or (viii) as winnings in a game of chance by government.

The term includes health-care insurance receivables.

The term does *not* include

> rights to payment evidenced by chattel paper or an instrument,

> commercial tort claims,

> deposit accounts,

> investment property,

> letter-of-credit rights or letters of credit, or

> rights to payment for money or funds advanced or sold, other than rights arising out of the use of a credit or charge card or information contained on or for use with the card.

Account debtor means a person obligated on an account, chattel paper, or general intangible.

The term does not include persons obligated to pay a negotiable instrument, even if the instrument constitutes part of chattel paper.

Accounting, except as used in "accounting for," means a record:

> (A) authenticated by a secured party;

> (B) indicating the aggregate unpaid secured obligations as of a date not more than 35 days earlier or 35 days later than the date of the record; and

> (C) identifying the components of the obligations in reasonable detail.

Agricultural lien means an interest in farm products:

>(A) which secures payment or performance of an obligation for:

>>(i) goods or services furnished in connection with a debtor's farming operation; or

>>(ii) rent on real property leased by a debtor in connection with its farming operation;

>(B) which is created by statute in favor of a person that:

>>(i) in the ordinary course of its business furnished goods or services to a debtor in connection with a debtor's farming operation; or

>>(ii) leased real property to a debtor in connection with the debtor's farming operation; and

>(C) whose effectiveness does not depend on the person's possession of the personal property.

As-extracted collateral means oil, gas, or other minerals subject to a security interest that:

>is created by a debtor having an interest in the minerals before extraction; and

>attaches to the minerals as extracted.

Authenticate means to sign or intently adopt a record, to attach to with the record an electronic sound, symbol, or process.

Cash proceeds mean money, checks, or deposit accounts.

Certificate of title means a statute provides the security interest to be indicated on the certificate as a condition of the security interest obtaining priority over a lien creditor's rights concerning the collateral.

The term includes another record maintained as an alternative to a certificate of title by the governmental unit that issues certificates of title if a statute permits the security interest to be indicated on the record because of the security interest's obtaining priority over the rights of a lien creditor concerning the collateral.

Chattel paper means a record evidencing a monetary obligation and a security interest in specific goods, a lease of specific goods, or license of software used in the goods.

Monetary obligation means a monetary obligation secured by the goods or owed under a lease of the goods and includes a monetary obligation for software used in the goods.

The term monetary obligation does *not* include:

a) charters or other contracts involving the use or hire of a vessel or

b) records that evidence a right to payment arising from using a credit or charge card or information contained for use with the card.

If a transaction is evidenced by records that include an instrument or series of instruments, the group of records taken together constitutes chattel paper.

Collateral means the property subject to a security interest or agricultural lien.

The term includes:

(A) proceeds to which a security interest attaches;

(B) accounts, chattel paper, and promissory notes that have been sold; and

(C) goods that are subject of a consignment.

Commercial tort claim means a claim arising in tort for which:

(A) the claimant is an organization; or

(B) the claimant is an individual, and the claim:

(i) arose in the course of the claimant's business or profession; and

(ii) does not include damages arising out of personal injury to or the death of an individual.

Commodity account means an account maintained by a commodity intermediary in which a commodity contract is carried for a commodity customer.

Commodity contract means a commodity futures contract, an option on a commodity futures contract, a commodity option, or another contract if the contract or option is:

(A) traded on or subject to the rules of a board of trade that has been designated as a contract market for such a contract under federal commodities laws; or

(B) traded on a foreign commodity board of trade, exchange, or market and is carried on the books of a commodity intermediary for a commodity customer.

Commodity customer means a person for which a commodity intermediary carries a commodity contract on its books.

Commodity intermediary means a person:

(A) registered as a futures commission merchant under federal commodities law; or

(B) in the ordinary course of its business provides settlement services for a board of trade designated as a contract market according to federal commodities law.

Communicate means:

> (A) to send a written or another tangible record;

> (B) to transmit a record by any means agreed upon by the persons sending and receiving the record; or

> (C) in the case of transmission of a record to or by a filing office, to transmit a record by any means prescribed by filing-office rule.

Consignee means a merchant to which goods are delivered in a consignment.

Consignment means a transaction, regardless of its form, in which a person delivers goods to a merchant for sale and:

> (A) the merchant:

>> (i) deals in goods of that kind under a name other than the name of the person making delivery;

>> (ii) is not an auctioneer; and

>> (iii) is not generally known by its creditors to be substantially engaged in selling the goods of others;

> (B) for each delivery, the aggregate value of the goods is $1,000 or more at delivery;

> (C) the goods are not consumer goods before delivery; and

> (D) the transaction does not create a security interest in an obligation.

Consignor means a person that delivers goods to a consignee in a consignment.

Consumer debtor means a debtor in a consumer transaction.

Consumer goods mean goods used or bought for use primarily for personal, family, or household purposes.

Consumer-goods transaction means a consumer transaction in which:

> (A) an individual incurs an obligation primarily for personal, family, or household purposes; and

> (B) a security interest in consumer goods secures the obligation.

Consumer obligor means an obligor who is an individual and who incurred the obligation as part of a transaction entered primarily for personal, family, or household purposes.

Consumer transaction means a transaction in which (i) an individual incurs an obligation primarily for personal purposes, (ii) a security interest secures the obligation, and (iii) the collateral is held primarily for personal purposes.

The term includes consumer-goods transactions.

Continuation statement means an amendment of a financing statement which:

(A) identifies, by file number, the initial financing statement to which it relates; and

(B) indicates that it is a continuation statement for, or that it is filed to continue the effectiveness of, the identified financing statement.

Debtor means:

(A) a person having an interest, other than a security interest in the collateral, whether or not the person is an obligor;

(B) a seller of accounts, chattel paper, payment intangibles, or promissory notes; or

(C) a consignee.

Deposit account means a demand, time, savings, passbook, or similar account maintained with a bank. The term does not include investment property or accounts evidenced by an instrument.

Document means a document of title or a receipt of the type described in Section 7-201(2).

Electronic chattel paper means chattel paper evidenced by a record consisting of information stored in an electronic medium.

Encumbrance means a right, other than an ownership interest, in real property. The term includes mortgages and other liens on real property.

Equipment means goods other than inventory, farm products, or consumer goods.

Farm products mean goods, other than standing timber, for which the debtor is engaged in a farming operation and which are:

(A) crops grown or to be grown, including:

(i) crops produced on trees, vines, and bushes; and

(ii) aquatic goods produced in aquacultural operations.

(B) livestock, born or unborn, including aquatic goods produced in aquacultural operations;

(C) supplies used or produced in a farming operation; or

(D) products of crops or livestock in their unmanufactured states.

Farming operation means raising, cultivating, propagating, fattening, grazing, or any other farming, livestock, or aquacultural operation.

File number means the number assigned to an initial financing statement.

Filing office means an office designated as the place to file a financing statement.

Filing-office rule means a rule adopted.

Financing statement means a record composed of an initial financing statement and any filed record relating to the initial financing statement.

Fixture filing means the filing of a financing statement covering goods that are to become fixtures.

The term includes the filing of a financing statement covering goods of a transmitting utility that are to become fixtures.

Fixture means goods that have become so related to real property that an interest in them arises under real property law.

General intangible means any personal property, other than accounts, chattel paper, commercial tort claims, deposit account, documents, goods, instruments, investment property, letters of credit, money, and oil, gas, or other minerals before extraction.

The term includes payment intangibles and software.

Good faith means honesty and using reasonable commercial standards of fair dealing.

Goods mean things that are movable when a security interest attaches.

The term includes (i) fixtures, (ii) standing timber that is to be cut and removed under a conveyance or contract for sale, (iii) the unborn young of animals, (iv) crops, even if the crops are produced on trees, vines, or bushes, and (v) manufactured homes.

The term goods includes a computer program embedded in goods and any supporting information provided in connection with a transaction relating to the program if:

> (i) the program is associated with the goods in such a manner that it customarily is considered part of the goods, or

> (ii) by becoming the owner of the goods, a person acquires a right to use the program in connection with the goods.

The term goods does not include a computer program embedded in goods that consist solely of the medium in which the program is embedded.

The term goods does not include accounts, chattel paper, commercial tort claims, deposit accounts, documents, general intangibles, instruments, investment property, letters of credit, money, or oil, gas, or other minerals before extraction.

Governmental unit means a subdivision, agency, department, county, parish, municipality, or another unit of the United States, a State, or a foreign country.

The term includes an organization having a separate corporate existence if the organization is eligible to issue debt with interest exempt from income taxation.

Health-care-insurance receivable means an interest in or claim under a policy of insurance which is a right to payment of a monetary obligation for health-care goods or services provided.

Instrument means a negotiable instrument or any other writing that evidences a right to the payment of a monetary obligation, is not itself a security agreement, and is of a type that in the ordinary course of business is transferred by delivery with any necessary endorsement.

The term does not include (i) investment property, (ii) letters of credit, or (iii) writings that evidence a right to payment arising from the use of a credit card.

Inventory means goods, other than farm products, which:

    (A) are leased by a person as lessor;

    (B) are held by a person for sale or lease or to be furnished under a contract of service;

    (C) are furnished by a person under a contract of service; or

    (D) consist of raw materials, work in process, or materials used or consumed in a business.

Investment property means security (certificated or uncertificated), security account, commodity contract, or commodity account.

Jurisdiction of organization (for a registered organization) means the jurisdiction under whose law the organization is organized.

Letter-of-credit right means a right to payment or performance under a letter of credit, whether the beneficiary has demanded or is at the time entitled to demand payment or performance.

The term does not include the right of a beneficiary to demand payment or performance under a letter of credit.

Lien creditor means:

    (A) a creditor that has acquired a lien on the property involved by attachment, levy;

    (B) an assignee for the benefit of creditors from the assignment;

    (C) a trustee in bankruptcy from the date of the filing of the petition; or

    (D) a receiver in equity from the time of appointment.

Manufactured home means a structure, transportable in one or more sections, which, in the traveling mode, is eight body feet or more in width or 40 body feet or more in length, or, when erected on site, is 320 or more square feet, and designed to be used as a dwelling when connected to the required utilities, and includes the plumbing, heating, air-conditioning, and electrical systems contained therein.

Manufactured-home transaction means a secured transaction:

> (A) that creates a purchase-money security interest in a manufactured home, other than a manufactured home held as inventory; or

> (B) in which a manufactured home, other than a manufactured home held as inventory, is the primary collateral.

Mortgage means a consensual interest in real property, including fixtures, which secures payment or performance of an obligation.

New debtor means a person that becomes bound as a debtor by a security agreement previously entered by another person.

New value means (i) money, (ii) money's worth in property, services, or new credit, or (iii) release by a transferee of an interest in property previously transferred to the transferee.

The term does not include an obligation substituted for another obligation.

Noncash proceeds mean proceeds other than cash proceeds.

Obligor means a person that, for an obligation secured by a security interest in an agricultural lien,

> (1) owes payment or performance of the obligation,

> > (ii) has provided property other than the collateral to secure payment or another performance of the obligation, or

> > (iii) is otherwise accountable for payment or other performance of the obligation.

The term does not include issuers (nominated persons) under a letter of credit.

Original debtor means a person that, as a debtor, entered into a security agreement to which a new debtor has become bound.

Payment intangible means a general intangible under which the account debtor's principal obligation is monetary.

Proceeds mean the following property:

> (A) whatever is acquired upon the sale, lease, license, exchange, or other disposition of collateral;

> (B) whatever is collected on, or distributed on account of, collateral;

> (C) rights arising out of collateral;

> (D) to the extent of the value of collateral, claims arising out of the loss, nonconformity, or interference with the use of, defects or infringement of rights in, or damage to, the collateral; or

> (E) to the extent of the value of the collateral and the extent payable to the debtor or the secured party, insurance payable because of the loss of, defects, or infringement of rights in, or damage to, the collateral.

Promissory note means an instrument evidencing a promise to pay a monetary obligation, does not evidence an order to pay, and does not contain an acknowledgment by a bank that the bank has received funds for the deposit.

Proposal means a record authenticated by a secured party, which includes the terms on which the secured party is willing to accept collateral in satisfaction of the obligation it secures.

Public-finance transaction means a secured transaction in connection with which:

> (A) debt securities are issued;

> (B) all or a portion of the securities issued have an initial stated maturity of at least 20 years; and

> (C) the debtor, obligor, secured party, account debtor, or other person obligated on collateral, assignor or assignee of a secured obligation, or assignor or assignee of a security interest is a State government.

Public organic record means a record that is available to the public for inspection and is:

> (A) a record consisting of the record initially filed with or issued by a State or the United States to form or organize an organization and any record filed with or issued by the State or the United States which amends or restates the initial record;

> (B) an organic record of a business trust consisting of the record initially filed with a State and records filed with the State which amends the initial record, if a statute of the State governing business trusts requires that the record be filed with the State; or

> (C) a record consisting of legislation enacted by the legislature of a State or the Congress which forms an organization, any record amending the legislation, and any record filed with or issued by the State or the United States which amends the name of the organization.

Pursuant to commitment means according to the secured party's obligation, whether a subsequent event of default or another event not within the secured party's control has relieved the secured party from its obligation.

Record, except as used in **for the record, of record, record or legal title**, and **record owner**, means information that is inscribed on a tangible medium or which is stored in an electronic medium and is retrievable in perceivable form.

Registered organization means an organization organized solely under the law of a single State or the United States by the filing of a public organic record with, or the enactment of legislation by the State or the United States.

The term registered organization includes a business trust that is formed under the law of a single State if a statute of the State governing business trusts requires that the business trust's organic record be filed with the State.

Secondary obligor means an obligor to the extent that:

> (A) the obligor's obligation is secondary; or

> (B) the obligor has a right of recourse for an obligation secured by collateral against the debtor, another obligor, or property of either.

Secured party means:

> (A) a person in whose favor a security interest is created or provided for under a security agreement, whether or not any obligation to be secured is outstanding;

> (B) a person that holds an agricultural lien;

> (C) a consignor;

> (D) a person to which accounts, chattel paper, payment intangibles, or promissory notes have been sold;

> (E) a trustee, indenture trustee, agent, or another representative in whose favor a security interest or agricultural lien is created.

Security Agreement means an agreement that creates a security interest.

Send, in connection with a record or notification, means:

> (A) to deposit in the mail, deliver for transmission, or transmit by other usual means of communication, with postage or cost of transmission provided for, addressed to any address reasonable under the circumstances; or

> (B) to cause the record or notification to be received within the time, it would have been received if sent under subparagraph (A).

Software means a computer program and supporting information provided in connection with a transaction relating to the program. The term does not include a computer program included in the definition of goods.

Supporting obligation means a letter-of-credit right or secondary obligation that supports an account's payment or performance, chattel paper, an instrument, or investment property.

Tangible chattel paper means chattel paper evidenced by a record or records consisting of information that is inscribed on a tangible medium.

Termination statement means an amendment of a financing statement which:

> (A) identifies, by its file number, the initial financing statement to which it relates; and

> (B) indicates that it is a termination statement or the identified financing statement is no longer effective.

Transmitting utility means a person primarily engaged in the business of:

> (A) operating a railroad, subway, street railway, or trolley bus;

> (B) transmitting communications electrically, electromagnetically, or by light;

> (C) transmitting goods by pipeline or sewer; or

> (D) producing or transmitting electricity, gas, steam, or water.

§ 9-103. PMSI; Application of Payments; Burden of Establishing

Purchase-money collateral means goods or software that secures a purchase-money obligation incurred for that collateral.

Purchase-money obligation means an obligation of an obligor incurred as part of the price of the collateral or for value given to enable the debtor to acquire rights in the collateral.

Purchase-money security interest (PMSI) in goods

A security interest in goods is a purchase-money security interest:

> 1) to the extent that the goods are purchase-money collateral for that security interest;

> 2) if the security interest is in inventory that is or was purchase-money collateral, to the extent that the security interest secures a purchase-money obligation incurred for other inventory that the secured party holds a purchase-money security interest; and

> 3) to the extent that the security interest secures a purchase-money obligation incurred for software in which the secured party holds or held a purchase-money security interest.

Purchase-money security interest in software

A security interest in software is a purchase-money security interest to the extent that the security interest secures a purchase-money obligation incurred for goods in which the secured party holds a purchase-money security interest if:

> 1) the debtor acquired its interest in the software in an integrated transaction in which it acquired an interest in the goods; and

> 2) the debtor acquired its interest in the software for the principal purpose of using the software in the goods.

Consignor's inventory purchase-money security interest

The security interest of a consignor in goods the subject of a consignment is a purchase-money security interest in inventory.

Application of payment in non-consumer-goods transactions

In a transaction other than a consumer-goods transaction, if the extent to which a security interest is a purchase-money security interest depends on the application of a payment to an obligation, the payment must be applied:

1) following any reasonable method of application to which the parties agree;

2) in the absence of the parties' agreement to a reasonable method, following any intention of the obligor manifested at or before the time of payment; or

3) in the absence of an agreement to a reasonable method and a timely manifestation of the obligor's intention, in the following order:

(A) to obligations not secured; and

(B) if more than one obligation is secured, to obligations secured by purchase-money security interests in the order in which those obligations were incurred.

Purchase-money security interest status in non-consumer-goods

In a transaction other than a consumer-goods transaction, a purchase-money security interest does *not* lose its status as such, even if:

1) the purchase-money collateral secures an obligation that is not a purchase-money obligation;

2) the collateral that is not purchase-money collateral secures the purchase-money obligation; or

3) the purchase-money obligation has been renewed, refinanced, consolidated, or restructured.

Burden of proof in non-consumer-goods transactions

In a transaction other than a consumer-goods transaction, a secured party claiming a purchase-money security interest has the burden of proving the extent of the security interest is a purchase-money security interest.

Non-consumer-goods transactions; no inference.

The limitation of the rules is intended to leave to the court to determine the proper rules in consumer-goods transactions.

The court may not infer from that limitation the proper rule in consumer-goods transactions and may apply established approaches.

§ 9-104. Control of Deposit Account

Requirements for control. A secured party has control of a deposit account if:

> 1) the secured party is the bank with which the deposit account is maintained;

> 2) the debtor, secured party, and bank have agreed in an authenticated record that the bank will comply with instructions originated by the secured party directing the disposition of funds in the deposit account without further consent by the debtor; or

> 3) the secured party becomes the bank's customer for the deposit account.

Debtor's right to direct disposition

A secured party with control, even if the debtor retains the right to direct the disposition of funds from the deposit account.

§ 9-105. Control of Electronic Chattel Paper

General rule: a secured party controls electronic chattel paper if a system evidencing the transfer of interests in the chattel paper establishes the secured party as the person to which the chattel paper was assigned.

Specific facts: a system satisfies subsection (a) if the record comprising the chattel paper are created, stored, and assigned in such a manner that:

> 1) a single authoritative copy of the record exists which is unique, identifiable, and except as otherwise provided;

> 2) the authoritative copy identifies the secured party as the assignee of the record;

> 3) the authoritative copy is communicated to and maintained by the secured party or its designated custodian;

> 4) copies or amendments that add or change an identified assignee of the authoritative copy can be made only with the consent of the secured party;

> 5) each copy of the authoritative copy is readily identifiable as a copy that is not the authoritative copy; and

> 6) any amendment of the authoritative copy is readily identifiable as authorized or unauthorized.

§ 9-106. Control of Investment Property

A person has control of a certificated security, uncertificated security, or security entitlement.

Control of commodity contract

A secured party has control of a commodity contract if:

> 1) the secured party is the commodity intermediary with which the commodity contract is carried; or

> 2) the commodity customer, secured party, and commodity intermediary have agreed that the commodity intermediary will apply value distributed on the commodity contract as directed by the secured party without further consent by the commodity customer.

Effect of control of securities account or commodity account

A secured party controlling security entitlements or commodity contracts carried in a securities account or commodity account has control over the account.

§ 9-107. Control of Letter-of-Credit Right

A secured party has control of a letter-of-credit right to the extent of any right to payment or performance by the issuer if the issuer has consented to an assignment of proceeds of the letter of credit or as applicable under law.

§ 9-108. Sufficiency of Description

A description of personal or real property is sufficient, whether or not it is specific if it reasonably identifies what is described.

Examples of reasonable identification

A description of collateral reasonably identifies the collateral if it identifies the collateral by:

> 1) specific listing;

> 2) category;

> 3) except as otherwise provided, a type of collateral defined;

> 4) quantity;

> 5) computational or allocational formula or procedure; or

> 6) any other method if the identity of the collateral is determinable.

Generic description not sufficient

A description of collateral as "all the debtor's assets" or "all the debtor's personal property" or using words of similar import does not reasonably identify the collateral.

Investment property

A description of a security entitlement, securities account, or commodity account is enough if it describes:

> 1) the collateral by those terms or as investment property; or
>
> 2) the underlying financial asset or commodity contract.

When description by type insufficient

A description only by the type of collateral is an insufficient description of:

> 1) a commercial tort claim; or
>
> 2) in a consumer transaction, consumer goods, a security entitlement, a securities account, or a commodity account.

Applicability of Article 9

§ 9-109. Scope

Except as otherwise provided, this article applies to:

> 1) a transaction that creates a security interest in personal property or fixtures by contract;
>
> 2) an agricultural lien;
>
> 3) a sale of accounts, chattel paper, payment intangibles, or promissory notes;
>
> 4) a consignment.

A security interest in secured obligations

Applying this article to a security interest in a secured obligation is not affected by the fact that the obligation is itself secured by a transaction or interest to which this article does not apply.

Extent to which the article does not apply

This article does not apply if:

> 1) a statute, regulation, or treaty of the U.S. preempts this article;
>
> 2) another statute of the State expressly governs the creation, perfection, priority, or enforcement of a security interest created by a governmental unit of this State;
>
> 3) a statute or governmental unit of another State or a foreign country; or
>
> 4) the rights of a transferee beneficiary or nominated person under a letter of credit are independent and superior.

Inapplicability of article

This article does not apply to:

> A landlord's lien, other than an agricultural lien;
>
> A lien, other than an agricultural lien, given by statute or rule of law, but Section 9-333 applies to the priority of the lien;
>
> A claim for wages, salary, or employee compensation;
>
> A sale of accounts, chattel paper, payment intangibles, or promissory notes as part of a sale of the business.
>
> An assignment of accounts, chattel paper, payment intangibles, or promissory notes which is for collection only;

An assignment of a right to payment under a contract to an assignee obligated to perform;

An assignment of a single account, payment intangible, or promissory note to an assignee for a preexisting indebtedness;

A transfer of an interest in or an assignment of a claim under a policy of insurance, other than an assignment by or to a healthcare provider of a healthcare-insurance receivable and any subsequent assignment of the right to payment;

Sections 9-315 and 9-322 apply to priorities in proceeds;

An assignment of a right represented by a judgment, other than a judgment taken on a right to payment that was collateral.

The creation or transfer of an interest in or lien on real property, including a lease or rents thereunder, except to the extent that provision is made for:

(A) liens on real property in Sections 9-203 and 9-308;

(B) fixtures in Section 9-334;

(C) fixture filings in Sections 9-501, 9-502, 9-512, and 9-519; and

(D) security agreements covering personal and real property.

§ 9-110. Security Interests Arising Under Article 2 or 2A

Before the debtor obtains possession of the goods:

1) the security interest is enforceable;

2) filing is not required to perfect the security interest;

3) the rights of the secured party after default by the debtor are governed by Article 2 or 2A; and

4) the security interest has priority over a conflicting security interest created by the debtor.

Validity of Security Agreements and Rights of Parties

§ 9-201. General Effectiveness of Security Agreement

A security agreement is effective according to its terms between the parties, against purchasers of the collateral, and creditors.

Applicable consumer laws and other laws

A transaction subject to this article is subject to applicable rule of law which establishes a different rule for consumers and insert a reference to (i) another statute or regulation that regulates the rates, charges, agreements, and practices for loans, credit sales, or other extensions of credit and (ii) any consumer-protection statute or regulation.

Other applicable law controls

In case of conflict between this article and a rule of law, statute, or regulation, the rule of law, statute, or regulation controls.

Failure to comply with a statute or regulation has only the effect the statute or regulation specifies.

Further deference to other applicable law

This article does not:

> 1) validate rate, charge, agreement, or practice that violates a rule of law, statute, or regulation described in subsection (b); or

> 2) extend the application of the rule of law, statute, or regulation to a transaction not otherwise subject to it.

§ 9-202. Title to Collateral Immaterial

The provisions of this article about rights and obligations apply whether title to collateral is in the secured party or the debtor.

§ 9-203. Attachment and Enforceability of Security Interest

A security interest attaches to collateral when it becomes enforceable against the debtor for the collateral unless an agreement expressly postpones the time of attachment.

Enforceability

A security interest is enforceable against the debtor and third parties for the collateral only if:

1) value has been given;

2) the debtor has rights in the collateral or the power to transfer rights in the collateral to a secured party; and

3) one of the following conditions is met:

(A) the debtor has authenticated a security agreement that describes the collateral and, if the security interest covers timber to be cut, a description of the land concerned;

(B) the collateral is not a certificated security and is in possession of secured party under debtor's security agreement;

(C) the collateral is a certificated security in registered form, and the security certificate has been delivered to the secured party; or

(D) the collateral is deposit accounts, electronic chattel paper, investment property, or letter-of-credit rights, and the secured party has control under the debtor's security agreement.

Other UCC provisions

Subsection (b) is subject to the security interest of a collecting bank, the security interest of a letter-of-credit issuer or nominated person, a security interest arising under Article 2 or 2A, and on security interests in investment property.

Bound by another's security agreement

A person becomes bound as debtor by a security agreement entered into by another person if, by operation of law other than this article or by contract:

1) the security agreement becomes effective to create a security interest in the person's property; or

2) the person becomes generally obligated for the obligations of the other person, including the obligation secured under the security agreement, and acquires or succeeds to all or substantially all the assets of the other person.

Effect of new debtor becoming bound

If a new debtor becomes bound as debtor by a security agreement entered by another person:

1) the agreement satisfies subsection (b)(3) for the existing or after-acquired property of the new debtor to the extent the property is described in the agreement; and

2) another agreement is not necessary to make a security interest in the property enforceable.

Proceeds and supporting obligations

The attachment of a security interest in collateral gives the secured party the rights to proceeds and is an attachment of a security interest in a supporting obligation for the collateral.

Lien securing payment rights

The attachment of a security interest in a right to payment or performance secured by a security interest on personal or real property is an attachment of a security interest in the security interest, mortgage, or another lien.

Security entitlement in a securities account

The attachment of a security interest in a securities account is an attachment of a security interest in the security entitlements carried in the securities account.

Commodity contracts in a commodity account

A security interest in a commodity account is an attachment of a security interest in the commodity contracts carried in the commodity account.

§ 9-204. After-Acquired Property; Future Advances

After-acquired collateral

A security agreement may create or provide for a security interest in after-acquired collateral.

After-acquired property clause not effective

A security interest does not attach under an after-acquired property clause to:

1) consumer goods, other than an accession as additional security unless the debtor acquires rights in them within ten days after the secured party gives value; or

2) a commercial tort claim.

Future advances and other value

A security agreement may provide that collateral secures, or that accounts, chattel paper, payment intangibles, or promissory notes are sold in connection with future advances or other value, whether or not the advances or value are given according to commitment.

§ 9-205. Use or Disposition of Collateral Permissible

Security interest not invalid or fraudulent

A security interest is not invalid or fraudulent against creditors solely because:

1) the debtor has the right or ability to:

(A) use, commingle, or dispose of all or part of the collateral, including returned or repossessed goods;

(B) collect, compromise, enforce, or deal with collateral;

(C) accept the return of collateral or make repossessions; or

(D) use, commingle, or dispose of proceeds; or

2) the secured party fails to require the debtor to account for proceeds or replace collateral.

Requirements of possession not relaxed

This section does not relax the requirements of possession if attachment, perfection, or enforcement of a security interest depends upon possession of the collateral by the secured party.

§ 9-206. Security Interest Arising in Purchase or Delivery of Financial Asset

A security interest in favor of a securities intermediary attaches to a person's security entitlement if:

1) the person buys a financial asset through the securities intermediary in a transaction in which the person is obligated to pay the purchase price to the securities intermediary at the time of the purchase; and

2) the securities intermediary credits the financial asset to the buyer's securities account before the buyer pays the securities intermediary.

Security interest secures an obligation to pay for a financial asset.

The security interest described secures the person's obligation to pay for the financial asset.

Security interest in payment against delivery

A security interest in favor of a person that delivers a certificated security or other financial asset represented by a writing attaches to the security or another financial asset if:

> 1) the security or another financial asset:
>
>> (A) in the ordinary course of business is transferred by delivery with any necessary indorsement or assignment; and
>>
>> (B) is delivered under an agreement between persons in the business of dealing with securities or financial assets; and
>
> 2) the agreement calls for delivery against payment.

Security interest secures an obligation to pay for delivery.

The security interest secures an obligation to make payment for the delivery.

§ 9-207. Rights and Duties from Possession or Control

Duty of care when secured party in possession

A secured party shall use reasonable care (*duty of care*) in the custody and preservation of collateral in the secured party's possession.

For chattel paper or an instrument, reasonable care includes taking necessary steps to preserve rights against prior parties unless otherwise agreed.

Expenses, risks, duties, and rights of secured party in possession

If a secured party has possession of collateral:

> 1) reasonable expenses, including the cost of insurance and payment of taxes or other charges, incurred in the custody, preservation, use, or operation of the collateral are chargeable to the debtor and are secured by the collateral;
>
> 2) the risk of accidental loss or damage is on the debtor to the extent of a deficiency of adequate insurance coverage;
>
> 3) the secured party shall keep the collateral identifiable, but fungible collateral may be commingled; and
>
> 4) the secured party may use or operate the collateral:
>
>> (A) to preserve the collateral or its value;
>>
>> (B) as permitted by order of a court having competent jurisdiction; or
>>
>> (C) except in the case of consumer goods, in the manner and to the extent agreed by the debtor.

Duties and rights when secured party in possession or control

A secured party having possession of collateral or control of collateral:

1) may hold as additional security any proceeds, except money or funds, received from the collateral;

2) shall apply money or funds received from the collateral to reduce the secured obligation, unless remitted to the debtor; and

3) may create a security interest in the collateral.

§ 9-208. Additional Duties of Secured Party Having Control

This section applies when there is no outstanding secured obligation, and the secured party is not committed to incur obligations or give value.

Duties of secured party after receiving debtor demand

Within 10 days after receiving an authenticated demand by the debtor:

1) a secured party having control of a deposit account shall send to the bank with which the deposit account is maintained an authenticated statement that releases the bank from the obligation to comply with instructions originated by the secured party;

2) a secured party having control of a deposit account shall:

(A) pay the debtor the balance on deposit in the deposit account; or

(B) transfer the balance on deposit into a deposit account in the debtor's name;

3) a secured party, other than a buyer, having control of electronic chattel paper shall:

(A) communicate the authoritative copy of the electronic chattel paper to the debtor or its designated custodian;

(B) if the debtor designates a custodian that is the designated custodian with which the authoritative copy of the electronic chattel paper is maintained for the secured party, communicate to the custodian an authenticated record releasing the designated custodian from further obligation to comply with instructions originated by the secured party and instructing the custodian to comply with instructions originated by the debtor; and

(C) take appropriate action to enable the debtor or its designated custodian to make copies of or revisions to the authoritative copy, which add or change an identified assignee of the authoritative copy without the consent of the secured party.

4) a secured party having control of investment property shall send to the securities intermediary or commodity intermediary with which the security entitlement or commodity contract is maintained an authenticated record that releases the securities intermediary or commodity intermediary from further obligation to comply with entitlement orders or directions originated by the secured party;

5) a secured party having control of a letter-of-credit right shall send to each person having an unfulfilled obligation to pay or deliver proceeds of the letter of credit to the secured party an authenticated release from further obligation to pay or deliver proceeds of the letter of credit to the secured party.

§ 9-209. Duties of Secured Party If Account Debtor Notified of Assignment

Except as otherwise provided, this section applies if:

1) there is no outstanding secured obligation; and

2) the secured party is not committed to incur obligations or give value.

Duties of secured party after receiving debtor demand

Within 10 days after receiving an authenticated demand by the debtor, a secured party shall send to an account debtor that has received notification of an assignment to the secured party as assignee under Section 9-406(a) an authenticated record that releases the account debtor from further obligation to the secured party.

§ 9-210. Request for Accounting; Statement of Account

Request for an accounting means a record authenticated by a debtor requesting that the recipient provide an accounting of the unpaid obligations secured by collateral and reasonably identifying the transaction or relationship that is the subject of the request.

Request regarding a list of collateral means a record authenticated by a debtor requesting that the recipient approve or correct a list of what the debtor believes to be the collateral securing an obligation and reasonably identifying the transaction or relationship that is the subject of the request.

Request regarding a statement of account means a record authenticated by a debtor requesting that the recipient approve or correct a statement indicating what the debtor believes to be the aggregate amount of unpaid obligations secured by collateral as of a specified date and reasonably identifying the transaction or relationship subject to the request.

Duty to respond to requests

A secured party, other than a buyer of accounts, chattel paper, payment intangibles, or promissory notes or a consignor, shall comply with a request within 14 days after receipt:

> 1) in the case of a request for an accounting, by authenticating and sending the debtor an accounting; and

> 2) in the case of a request for a list of collateral or a request regarding a statement of account, by authenticating and sending the debtor an approval or correction.

Request regarding the list and type of collateral

A secured party that claims a security interest in a particular type of collateral owned by the debtor may comply with a request regarding a list of collateral by sending the debtor an authenticated record, including a statement to that effect within 14 days after receipt.

Request regarding the list of collateral; no interest claimed

A person that receives a request regarding a list of collateral, claims no interest in the collateral when it receives the request, and claimed an interest in the collateral at an earlier time shall comply with the request within 14 days after receipt by sending the debtor an authenticated record:

> 1) disclaiming any interest in the collateral; and

> 2) if known to the recipient, providing the name and mailing address of any assignee or successor to the recipient's interest in the collateral.

Request for accounting; no interest in obligation claimed

A person that receives a request for an accounting or a request regarding a statement of account, claims no interest in the obligations when it receives the request, and claimed an interest in the obligations at an earlier time shall comply with the request within 14 days after receipt by sending the debtor an authenticated record:

> 1) disclaiming any interest in the obligations; and

> 2) if known to the recipient, providing the name and mailing address of the assignee or successor to the recipient's interest in the obligations.

Charges for responses

A debtor is entitled without charge to one response to a request under this section during any six months.

The secured party may require payment not exceeding $25 for each additional response.

Perfection and Priority

§ 9-301. Perfection and Priority of Security Interests

The following rules determine the law governing perfection, the effect of perfection or nonperfection, and the priority of a security interest in collateral:

While a debtor is in a jurisdiction, the local law of that jurisdiction governs perfection, the effect of perfection or nonperfection, and the priority of a security interest in the collateral.

While collateral is in a jurisdiction, the local law of that jurisdiction governs perfection, the effect of perfection or nonperfection, and the priority of a possessory security interest in that collateral.

While negotiable documents, goods, instruments, or the tangible chattel paper is in a jurisdiction, the local law of that jurisdiction governs:

> (A) the perfection of a security interest in the goods by filing a fixture filing;

> (B) the perfection of a security interest in timber to be cut; and

> (C) the effect of perfection or nonperfection and the priority of a nonpossessory security interest in the collateral.

The local law of the jurisdiction in which the wellhead or minehead is located governs perfection, the effect of perfection or nonperfection, and the priority of a security interest in as-extracted collateral.

§ 9-308. Continuity of Security Interest or Agricultural Lien Perfected

Perfection of security interest

A security interest is perfected if it has attached, and the applicable requirements for perfection have been satisfied.

A security interest is perfected when it attaches if the applicable requirements are satisfied before the security interest attaches.

Perfection of an agricultural lien

An agricultural lien is perfected if it has become effective, and the applicable requirements for perfection have been satisfied.

An agricultural lien is perfected when it becomes effective if the applicable requirements are satisfied before the agricultural lien becomes effective.

Continuous perfection by different methods

A security interest or agricultural lien is perfected continuously if it is originally perfected by one method under this article and is later perfected by another method, without an intermediate period when it was unperfected.

Supporting obligation

The perfection of a security interest in collateral perfects a security interest in a supporting obligation for the collateral.

Lien securing the right to payment

The perfection of a security interest in a right to payment or performance perfects a security interest in a security interest, mortgage on personal or real property securing the right.

Security entitlement carried in a securities account

The perfection of a security interest in a securities account perfects a security interest in the security entitlements carried in the securities account.

Commodity contracts carried in a commodity account

The perfection of a security interest in a commodity account perfects a security interest in the commodity contracts carried in the commodity account.

§ 9-309. Security Interest Perfected Upon Attachment

The following security interests are perfected when they attach:

1) a purchase-money security interest in consumer goods, except as provided for consumer goods subject to a statute or treaty.

2) an assignment of accounts or payment intangibles which does not by itself or in conjunction with other assignments to the same assignee transfer a significant part of the assignor's outstanding accounts or payment intangibles;

3) a sale of a payment intangible;

4) a sale of a promissory note;

5) a security interest created by the assignment of a health-care-insurance receivable to the provider of the health-care goods or services;

6) a security interest until the debtor takes possession of the collateral;

7) a security interest of a collecting bank;

8) a security interest of an issuer or nominated person;

9) a security interest arising in the delivery of a financial asset;

10) a security interest in investment property created by a broker or securities intermediary;

11) a security interest in a commodity contract or a commodity account created by a commodity intermediary;

12) an assignment for the benefit of creditors of the transferor and subsequent transfers by the assignee thereunder; and

13) a security interest created by an assignment of a beneficial interest in a decedent's estate.

§ 9-310. Security Interests and Agricultural Liens Without Filing Provisions

Except as otherwise provided, a financing statement must be filed to perfect security interests and agricultural liens.

Exceptions: filing not necessary

The filing of a financing statement is not necessary to perfect a security interest:

1) that is perfected under Section 9-308(d), (e), (f), or (g);

2) that is perfected under Section 9-309 when it attaches;

3) in property subject to a statute, regulation, or treaty;

4) in goods in possession of a bailee which is perfected;

5) in certificated securities, documents, goods, or instruments which is perfected without filing or possession;

6) in collateral in the secured party's possession;

7) in certificated security, which is perfected by delivery of the security certificate to the secured party;

8) in deposit accounts, electronic chattel paper, investment property, or letter-of-credit rights, which is perfected by control;

9) in proceeds that are perfected.

Assignment of perfected security interest

If a secured party assigns a perfected security interest or agricultural lien, a filing under this article is not required to continue the perfected status of the security interest against creditors of and transferees from the original debtor.

§ 9-311. Perfection Subject to Statutes, Regulations, And Treaties

Security interests subject to other laws

The filing of a financing statement is not necessary to perfect a security interest in property subject to:

> 1) a statute, regulation, or treaty of the U.S. whose requirements for a security interest obtains priority over the rights of a lien creditor for the property preempt;

> 2) any statute covering automobiles, trailers, mobile homes, boats, farm tractors, or the like, which provides for a security interest to be indicated on a certificate of title as a condition of perfection, and any non-UCC central filing statute; or

> 3) a statute of another jurisdiction that provides for a security interest to be indicated on a certificate of title as a condition of the security interest's obtaining priority over the rights of a lien creditor for the property.

Compliance with other law

Compliance with the requirements of a statute, regulation, or treaty for obtaining priority over the rights of a lien creditor is equivalent to the filing of a financing statement under this article.

A security interest in property subject to a statute, regulation, or treaty may be perfected only by compliance with those requirements.

A security interest so perfected remains perfected notwithstanding a change in the use or transfer of possession of the collateral.

Duration and renewal of perfection

Duration and renewal of perfection of a security interest perfected by compliance with the requirements prescribed by a statute, regulation, or treaty are governed by the statute, regulation, or treaty.

Inapplicability to certain inventory

During any period in which collateral subject to a statute specified is inventory held for sale or lease by a person or leased by that person as lessor, and that person is in the business of selling goods of that kind, this section does not apply to a security interest in that collateral.

§ 9-312. Perfection Without Filing or Transfer of Possession

The following section addresses perfection of Security Interests in Chattel Paper, Deposit Accounts, Documents, Goods Covered by Documents, Instruments, Investment Property, Letter-Of-Credit Rights, And Money; Perfection by Permissive Filing; Temporary Perfection Without Filing or Transfer of Possession.

Perfection by filing permitted

A security interest in chattel paper, negotiable documents, instruments, or investment property may be perfected by filing.

Control or possession of certain collateral

Except as otherwise provided for proceeds:

> 1) a security interest in a deposit account may be perfected only by control;

> 2) and except as otherwise provided, a security interest in a letter-of-credit right may be perfected only by control; and

> 3) a security interest in money may be perfected only by the secured party taking possession.

Goods covered by the negotiable document

Goods in possession of a bailee who issued a negotiable document covering the goods:

> 1) a security interest in the goods may be perfected by perfecting a security interest in the document; and

> 2) a security interest perfected in the document has priority over any security interest that becomes perfected in the goods by another method during that time.

Goods covered by the nonnegotiable document

While goods are in possession of a bailee that has issued a nonnegotiable document covering the goods, a security interest in the goods may be perfected by:

> 1) issuance of a document in the name of the secured party;

> 2) the bailee's receipt of the secured party's interest; or

> 3) filing as to the goods.

Temporary perfection: new value

A security interest in certificated securities, negotiable documents, or instruments is perfected without filing or the taking of possession for 20 days from the time it attaches to the extent that it arises for new value given under an authenticated security agreement.

Temporary perfection: goods or documents made available

A perfected security interest in a negotiable document or goods in possession of a bailee, other than one that has issued a negotiable document for the goods, remains perfected for 20 days without filing if the secured party makes available to the debtor the goods or documents representing the goods for:

> 1) ultimate sale or exchange; or

> 2) loading, unloading, storing, shipping, transshipping, manufacturing, processing, or otherwise dealing with them in a manner preliminary to their sale or exchange.

Temporary perfection: delivery of security certificate or instrument

A perfected security interest in a certificated security or instrument remains perfected for 20 days without filing if the secured party delivers the security certificate or instrument to the debtor for:

> 1) ultimate sale or exchange; or

> 2) presentation, collection, renewal, or registration of transfer.

Expiration of temporary perfection

After 20 days, perfection depends upon compliance with this article.

§ 9-313. Possession or Delivery Without Filing

Perfection by possession or delivery

A secured party may perfect a security interest in negotiable documents, goods, instruments, money, or tangible chattel paper by taking possession of the collateral.

A secured party may perfect a security interest in certificated securities by taking delivery of the certificated securities.

Goods covered by a certificate of title

For goods covered by a certificate of title issued by this State, a secured party may perfect a security interest in the goods by taking possession of the goods only in the circumstances described in Section 9-316(d).

Collateral in possession of a person other than the debtor

For collateral other than certificated securities and goods covered by a document, a secured party takes possession of collateral in possession of a person other than the debtor, the secured party, or a lessee of the collateral from the debtor in the ordinary course of the debtor's business, when:

1) the person in possession authenticates a record acknowledging that it holds the collateral for the secured party's benefit; or

2) the person takes possession of the collateral after
having authenticated a record acknowledging that it will hold possession of collateral for the secured party's benefit.

Time of perfection by possession; continuation of perfection

If perfection of a security interest depends upon possession of the collateral by a secured party, perfection occurs no earlier than the time the secured party takes possession and continues while the secured party retains possession.

Time of perfection by delivery; continuation of perfection

A security interest in a certificated security in registered form is perfected by delivery when delivery of the certificated security occurs and remains perfected until the debtor obtains possession of the security certificate.

Acknowledgment not required

A person in possession of collateral is not required to acknowledge that it holds possession for a secured party's benefit.

Effectiveness of acknowledgment; no duties or confirmation

If a person acknowledges possession for the secured party's benefit:

1) the acknowledgment is effective, even if the acknowledgment violates the rights of a debtor; and

2) unless the person otherwise agrees or law other than this article provides, the person does not owe a duty to the secured party and is not required to confirm the acknowledgment to another person.

Secured party's delivery to a person other than the debtor

A secured party having possession of collateral does not relinquish possession by delivering the collateral to a person other than the debtor or a lessee of the collateral from the debtor in the ordinary course of the debtor's business if the person was instructed before the delivery or is instructed contemporaneously with the delivery:

> 1) to possess the collateral for the secured party's benefit; or

> 2) to redeliver the collateral to the secured party.

Effect of delivery under subsection (h); no duties or confirmation

A secured party does not relinquish possession, even if a delivery under subsection (h) violates the rights of a debtor.

A person to which collateral is delivered does not owe a duty to the secured party and is not required to confirm the delivery to another person unless the person otherwise agrees or law other than this article otherwise provides.

§ 9-314. Perfection by Control

A security interest in investment property, deposit accounts, letter-of-credit rights, or electronic chattel paper may be perfected by control of the collateral.

Specified collateral: time of perfection by control; continuation of perfection

A security interest in deposit accounts, electronic chattel paper, or letter-of-credit rights is perfected by control when the secured party obtains control and remains perfected by control only while the secured party retains control.

Investment property: time of perfection by control; continuation of perfection

A security interest in investment property is perfected by control from the time the secured party obtains control and remains perfected by control until:

> 1) the secured party does not have control; and

> 2) one of the following occurs:

>> (A) if the collateral is a certificated security, the debtor has or acquires possession of the security certificate;

>> (B) if the collateral is an uncertificated security, the issuer has registered the debtor as the registered owner; or

>> (C) if the collateral is a security entitlement, the debtor is or becomes the entitlement holder.

§ 9-315. Secured Party's Rights on Disposition and In Proceeds

Disposition of collateral: continuation of security interest or agricultural lien; proceeds

1) a security interest or agricultural lien continues in collateral notwithstanding sale, lease, license, exchange, or other disposition thereof unless the secured party authorized the disposition free of the security interest or agricultural lien; and

2) a security interest attaches to identifiable proceeds of collateral.

When commingled proceeds identifiable

Proceeds commingled with other property are identifiable:

1) if the proceeds are goods, as provided by Section 9-336; and

2) if the proceeds are not goods, to the extent that the secured party identifies the proceeds by a method of tracing, including equitable principles, that is permitted under law other than this article for the commingled property of the type involved.

The perfection of a security interest in proceeds

A security interest in proceeds would be a perfected security interest if the security interest in the original collateral was perfected.

Continuation of perfection

A perfected security interest in proceeds becomes unperfected on the 21st day after the security interest attaches to the proceeds unless:

1) the following conditions are satisfied:

(A) a filed financing statement covers the original collateral;

(B) the proceeds are collateral in which a security interest may be perfected by filing in the office in which the financing statement has been filed; and

(C) the proceeds are not acquired with cash proceeds;

2) the proceeds are identifiable cash proceeds; or

3) the security interest in the proceeds is perfected other than under subsection (c) when the security interest attaches to the proceeds or within 20 days.

When perfected security interest in proceeds becomes unperfected

If a filed financing statement covers the original collateral, a security interest
in proceeds remaining perfected under subsection (d)(1) becomes unperfected at the latter of:

> 1) when the effectiveness of the filed financing statement lapses or is terminated; or

> 2) the 21st day after the security interest attaches to the proceeds.

§ 9-316. Perfection Following Change in Governing Law

General rule: effect on the perfection of change in governing law

A security interest perfected according to the law of the jurisdiction designated remains perfected until the earliest of:

> 1) the time perfection would have ceased under the law of that jurisdiction;

> 2) the expiration of four months after a change of the debtor's location to another jurisdiction; or

> 3) the expiration of one year after a transfer of collateral to a person that thereby becomes a debtor and is in another jurisdiction.

Security interest perfected or unperfected under law of new jurisdiction

If a security interest described in subsection (a) becomes perfected under the law of the other jurisdiction before the earliest event described in that subsection, it remains perfected.

If the security interest does not become perfected under the law of the other jurisdiction before the earliest time or event, it becomes unperfected and is deemed never to have been perfected as against a purchaser of the collateral.

Possessory security interest in collateral moved to a new jurisdiction

A possessory security interest in collateral, other than goods covered by a certificate of title and as-extracted collateral consisting of goods, remains continuously perfected if:

> 1) the collateral is located in one jurisdiction and subject to a security interest perfected under the law of that jurisdiction;

> 2) thereafter the collateral is brought into another jurisdiction; and

> 3) upon entry into the other jurisdiction, the security interest is perfected under the law of the other jurisdiction.

Goods covered by a certificate of title from another state

A security interest in goods covered by a certificate of title which is perfected by a method under the law of another jurisdiction when the goods become covered by a certificate of title from the new state remains perfected until the security interest would have become unperfected under the law of the other jurisdiction had the goods not become so covered.

When security interest becomes unperfected against purchasers

A security interest described in subsection (d) becomes unperfected as against a purchaser of the goods for value and is deemed never to have been perfected as against a purchaser of the goods for value if the applicable requirements for perfection are not satisfied before the earlier of the:

> 1) time the security interest would have become unperfected under the law of the other jurisdiction had the goods not become covered by a certificate of title from this State; or

> 2) expiration of four months after the goods had become so covered.

Change in the jurisdiction of the bank, issuer, nominated person or intermediary

A security interest in deposit accounts, letter-of-credit rights, or investment property which is perfected under the law of the bank's jurisdiction, the issuer's jurisdiction, or the securities intermediary's jurisdiction, as applicable, remains perfected until the earlier of:

> 1) the time the security interest would have become unperfected under the law of that jurisdiction; or

> 2) the expiration of four months after a change of the applicable jurisdiction to another jurisdiction.

Effect on filed financing statement for changes in governing law

The following rules apply to collateral to which a security interest attaches within four months after the debtor changes to another jurisdiction:

> 1) A financing statement filed before the change according to the law of the jurisdiction designated is effective to perfect a security interest in the collateral if the financing statement would have been effective to perfect a security interest in the collateral had the debtor not changed its location.

> 2) If a security interest becomes perfected under the law of the other jurisdiction before the earlier of the time or the end of the period described in that subsection, it remains perfected.

If the security interest does not become perfected under the law of the other jurisdiction before the earlier of that time or the end of that period, it becomes unperfected and is deemed never to have been perfected as against a purchaser of the collateral.

Governing law changes on financing statements filed against the original debtor

If a financing statement naming an original debtor is filed under the jurisdiction and a new debtor is in another jurisdiction, the following apply:

1) The financing statement is effective to perfect a security interest in collateral acquired by the new debtor within four months, the new debtor becomes bound, if the financing statement would have been effective to perfect a security interest in the collateral had the collateral been acquired by the original debtor.

2) A security interest perfected by the financing statement and which becomes perfected under the law of the other jurisdiction before the earlier of the time the financing statement would have become ineffective under the law of the jurisdiction designated or the expiration of the four months remains perfected.

A security interest that is perfected by the financing statement, but which does not become perfected under the law of the other jurisdiction before the earlier time or event becomes unperfected and is deemed never to have been perfected as against a purchaser of the collateral.

§ 9-317. Priority Over Unperfected Interest or Agricultural Lien

Conflicting security interests and rights of lien creditors

A security interest or agricultural lien is subordinate to the rights of:

1) a person entitled to priority under Section 9-322; and

2) a person that becomes a lien creditor before the earlier of::

(A) the security interest or agricultural lien is perfected; or

(B) one of the conditions specified is met, and a financing statement covering the collateral is filed.

Buyers that receive delivery

A buyer, other than a secured party, of tangible chattel paper, documents, goods, or certificated security takes free of a security interest or agricultural lien if the buyer gives value and receives delivery of the collateral without knowledge of the security interest or agricultural lien and before it is perfected.

Lessees that receive delivery

A lessee of goods takes free of a security interest or agricultural lien if the lessee gives value and receives delivery of the collateral without knowledge of the security interest or agricultural lien and before it is perfected.

Licensees and buyers of certain collateral

A licensee of a general intangible or a buyer, other than a secured party, collateral other than tangible chattel paper, documents, goods, or certificated security takes free of a security interest if the licensee or buyer gives value without knowledge of the security interest and before it is perfected.

Purchase-money security interest

If a person files a financing statement for a purchase-money security interest within 20 days after the debtor receives delivery of the collateral, the security interest takes priority over the rights of a buyer, lessee, or lien creditor, which arise between the time the security interest attaches and the time of filing.

§ 9-322. Priorities Among Conflicting Interests on Same Collateral

Priority among conflicting security interests and agricultural liens in the same collateral is determined according to the following rules:

> 1) Conflicting perfected security interests and agricultural liens rank according to priority in time of filing or perfection.

Priority dates from the earlier of the time a filing covering the collateral is first made, or the security interest or agricultural lien is first perfected if there is no period after that when there is neither filing nor perfection.

> 2) A perfected security interest or agricultural lien has priority over a conflicting unperfected security interest or agricultural lien.

> 3) The first security interest or agricultural lien to attach or become effective has priority if conflicting security interests and agricultural liens are unperfected.

Time of perfection: proceeds and supporting obligations

1) the time of filing or perfection as to a security interest in collateral is the time of filing or perfection as to a security interest in proceeds; and

2) the time of filing or perfection as to a security interest in collateral supported by a supporting obligation is the time of filing or perfection as to a security interest in the supporting obligation.

Special priority rules: proceeds and supporting obligations

A security interest in collateral that qualifies for priority over a conflicting security interest has priority over a conflicting security interest in:

1) any supporting obligation for the collateral; and

2) proceeds of the collateral if:

> (A) the security interest in proceeds is perfected;

> (B) the proceeds are cash proceeds or of the same type as the collateral; and

> (C) in the case of proceeds, all intervening proceeds are cash proceeds, proceeds of the same type as the collateral, or an account relating to the collateral.

First-to-file priority rule for certain collateral

If a security interest in chattel paper, deposit accounts, negotiable documents, instruments, investment property, or letter-of-credit rights is perfected by a method other than filing, conflicting perfected security interests in proceeds of the collateral rank according to priority in time of filing.

Priority under agricultural lien statute

A perfected agricultural lien on collateral has priority over a conflicting security interest in or agricultural lien on the same collateral if the statute creating the agricultural lien provides.

§ 9-323. Future Advances

When priority based on time of the advance

To determine the priority of a perfected security interest, perfection of the security interest dates from the time an advance is made to the extent that the security interest secures an advance that:

> 1) is made while the security interest is perfected only:
>
>> (A) under Section 9-309 when it attaches; or
>>
>> (B) temporarily under Section 9-312; and
>
> 2) is not made according to a commitment entered before or while the security interest is perfected by a method other than under Section 9-309 or 9-312.

Lien creditor

A security interest is subordinate to the rights of a lien creditor to the extent that the security interest secures an advance made more than 45 days after the person becomes a lien creditor unless the advance is made:

> 1) without knowledge of the lien; or
>
> 2) according to a commitment without knowledge of the lien.

Buyer of receivables

Subsections do not apply to a security interest held by a secured party that is a buyer of accounts, chattel paper, payment intangibles, promissory notes, or a consignor.

Buyer of goods

A buyer of goods other than a buyer in the ordinary course of business takes free of a security interest to the extent that it secures advances made after the earlier of:

> 1) the time the secured party acquires knowledge of the buyer's purchase; or
>
> 2) 45 days after the purchase.

Advances made according to commitment: priority of buyer of goods

Subsection (d) does not apply if the advance is made according to a commitment entered without knowledge of the buyer's purchase and before the expiration of the 45 days.

Lessee of goods

A lessee of goods, other than a lessee in the ordinary course of business, takes the leasehold interest that is free of a security interest to the extent that it secures advances made after the earlier of:

> 1) the time the secured party acquires knowledge of the lease; or

> 2) 45 days after the lease contract becomes enforceable.

Advances made according to commitment: priority of lessee of goods

Subsection (f) does not apply if the advance is made according to a commitment entered without knowledge of the lease and before the expiration of the 45 days.

§ 9-324. Priority of Purchase-Money Security Interests

A perfected purchase-money security interest in goods other than inventory or livestock has priority over a conflicting security interest in the same goods, and a perfected security interest in its identifiable proceeds has priority if the purchase-money security interest is perfected when the debtor receives possession of the collateral or within 20 days.

Inventory purchase-money priority

A perfected purchase-money security interest in inventory has priority over a conflicting security interest in the same.

A perfected purchase-money security interest has priority over a conflicting security interest in chattel paper or instrument constituting proceeds of the inventory and in proceeds of the chattel paper.

A perfected purchase-money security interest has priority in identifiable cash proceeds of the inventory to the extent the identifiable cash proceeds are received on or before the delivery of the inventory to a buyer, if:

> 1) the purchase-money security interest is perfected when the debtor receives possession of the inventory;

> 2) the purchase-money secured party sends an authenticated notification to the holder of the conflicting security interest;

> 3) the holder of the conflicting security interest receives the notification within five years before the debtor receives possession of the inventory; and

> 4) the notification states that the person sending the notification has or expects to acquire a purchase-money security interest in the inventory of the debtor and describes the inventory.

Holders of conflicting inventory security interests to be notified

Subsections apply only if the holder of the conflicting security interest had filed a financing statement covering the same types of inventory:

1) if the purchase-money security interest is perfected by filing, before the date of the filing; or

2) if the purchase-money security interest is temporarily perfected without filing or possession before the beginning of the 20 days.

Livestock purchase-money priority

A perfected purchase-money security interest in livestock that is farm products has priority over a conflicting security interest in the same livestock, a perfected security interest in their identifiable proceeds and products in their unmanufactured states has priority, if:

1) the purchase-money security interest is perfected when the debtor receives possession of the livestock;

2) the purchase-money secured party sends an authenticated notification to the holder of the conflicting security interest;

3) the holder of the conflicting security interest receives the notification within six months before the debtor receives possession of the livestock; and

4) the notification states that the person sending the notification has or expects to acquire a purchase-money security interest in livestock of the debtor and describes the livestock.

Holders of conflicting livestock security interests to be notified

Subsections (d)(2) through (4) apply if the holder of the conflicting security interest had filed a financing statement covering the same types of livestock:

1) if the purchase-money security interest is perfected by filing, before the date of the filing; or

2) if the purchase-money security interest is temporarily perfected without filing or possession before the beginning of the 20 days.

Software purchase-money priority

A perfected purchase-money security interest in software has priority over a conflicting interest in the same collateral.

A perfected security interest in its identifiable proceeds has priority, to the extent that the purchase-money security interest in the goods in which the software was acquired has priority in the goods and proceeds of the goods.

Conflicting purchase-money security interests

A security interest securing an obligation incurred as all or part of the price of the collateral has priority over a security interest securing an obligation incurred for value given to enable the debtor to acquire rights in or the use of collateral; and in other cases, applies to the qualifying security interests.

§ 9-325. Priority of Security Interests in Transferred Collateral

Subordination of security interest in transferred collateral

A security interest created by a debtor is subordinate to a security interest in the same collateral created by another person if:

1) the debtor acquired the collateral subject to the security interest created by the other person;

2) the security interest created by the other person was perfected when the debtor acquired the collateral; and

3) there is no period after that when the security interest is unperfected.

Subsection (a) subordinates a security interest only if the security interest:

1) would have priority solely under Section 9-322(a) or 9-324; or

2) arose solely under Section 2-711(3) or 2A-508(5).

§ 9-326. Priority of Security Interests Created by New Debtor

Subordination of security interest created by a new debtor

A security interest created by a new debtor in which the new debtor has or acquires rights and is perfected solely by a filed financing statement that would be ineffective to perfect the security interest but for the application of Section 9-316(i)(1) or 9-508 is subordinate to a security interest in the collateral which is perfected other than by a filed financing statement.

Priority under other provisions; multiple original debtors

The other provisions determine the priority among conflicting security interests in the same collateral perfected by filed financing statements.

If the security agreements to which a new debtor became bound as debtor were not entered into by the original debtor, the conflicting security interests rank according to priority in time of the new debtor's having become bound.

§ 9-327. Priority of Security Interests in Deposit Accounts

Rules governing priority among conflicting security interests in the same deposit account:

1) A security interest held by a secured party having control of the deposit account has priority over a conflicting security interest.

2) A security interests perfected by control rank according to priority in time of obtaining control.

3) A security interest held by the bank with which the deposit account is maintained has priority over a conflicting security interest held by another secured party.

4) A security interest perfected by control has priority over a security interest held by the bank with the deposit account.

§ 9-328. Priority of Security Interests in Investment Property

Rules governing priority among conflicting security interests in the same investment property:

1) A security interest held by a secured party controlling investment property has priority over a security interest held by a secured party that does not have control of the investment property.

2) Except as otherwise provided, conflicting security interests held by secured parties, each of which has control rank according to priority in time of:

(A) if the collateral is a security, obtaining control;

(B) if the collateral is a security entitlement carried in a securities account and:

(i) if the secured party obtained control, the secured party becomes the person for which the securities account is maintained;

(ii) if the secured party obtained control under Section 8-106(d)(2), the securities intermediary's agreement to comply with the secured party's entitlement orders for security entitlements carried or to be carried in the securities account; or

(iii) if the secured party obtained control through another person under Section 8-106(d)(3), the time for priority would be based under this paragraph if the other person were the secured party; or

(C) if the collateral is a commodity contract with a commodity intermediary, the satisfaction of the requirement for control specified in Section 9-106(b)(2) for commodity contracts carried with the commodity intermediary.

3) A security interest held by a securities intermediary in a security entitlement or securities account maintained with the securities intermediary has priority over a conflicting security interest held by another secured party.

4) A security interest held by a commodity intermediary in a commodity contract or a commodity account maintained with the commodity intermediary has priority over a conflicting security interest held by another secured party.

5) A security interest in a certificated security in registered form perfected by taking delivery under Section 9-313(a) and not by control under Section 9-314 has priority over a conflicting security interest perfected by a method other than control.

6) Conflicting security interests created by a broker, securities intermediary, or commodity intermediary, perfected without control rank equally.

7) In all other cases, priority among conflicting security interests in investment property is governed by Sections 9-322 and 9-323.

§ 9-329. Priority of Security Interests in Letter-of-Credit Right

Rules governing priority among conflicting security interests in the same letter-of-credit right:

1) A security interest held by a secured party controlling the letter-of-credit right has priority over a conflicting security interest held by a secured party that does not have control.

2) Security interests perfected by control rank according to priority in time of obtaining control.

§ 9-331. Priority of Interests Under Other Articles; Under Article 8

Rights under Articles 3, 7, and 8 not limited

This article does not limit the rights of a holder in due course of a negotiable instrument, a holder to which a negotiable document of title has been duly negotiated, or a protected purchaser of a security.

These holders or purchasers take priority over an earlier security interest, even if perfected, to the extent provided in Articles 3, 7, and 8.

Protection under Article 8

This article does not limit the rights or impose liability to persons protected against the assertion of a claim under Article 8.

Filing does not constitute notice

Filing under this article does not constitute notice of a claim or defense to the holders, or purchasers, or persons described in subsections (a) and (b).

§ 9-333. Priority of Certain Liens Arising by Operation of Law

Possessory lien means an interest, other than a security interest or an agricultural lien:

> 1) which secures payment or performance of an obligation for services or materials furnished for goods by a person in the ordinary course of the person's business;
>
> 2) which is created by statute or law in favor of the person; and
>
> 3) whose effectiveness depends on the possession of the goods.

Priority of possessory lien

A possessory lien on goods has priority over a security interest in the goods unless the lien is created by a statute that expressly provides otherwise.

§ 9-334. Priority of Security Interests in Fixtures and Crops

A security interest under this article may be created in goods that are fixtures or may continue in goods that become fixtures.

A security interest does not exist under this article in ordinary building materials incorporated into an improvement on land.

Security interest in fixtures under real property law

This article does not prevent the creation of an encumbrance upon fixtures under real property law.

General rule: the subordination of security interest in fixtures

A security interest in fixtures is subordinate to a conflicting interest of an encumbrancer or owner of the related real property other than the debtor.

Fixtures purchase-money priority

A perfected security interest in fixtures has priority over a conflicting interest of an encumbrancer or owner of the real property if the debtor has an interest of record in or is in possession of the real property and:

1) the security interest is a purchase-money security interest;

2) the interest of the encumbrancer or owner arises before the goods become fixtures; and

3) the security interest is perfected by a fixture filing before the goods become fixtures or within 20 days after that.

Priority of security interest in fixtures over interests in real property

A perfected security interest in fixtures has priority over a conflicting interest of an encumbrancer or owner of the real property if:

1) the debtor has an interest of record in the real property or is in possession of the real property and the security interest:

(A) is perfected by a fixture filing before the interest of the encumbrancer or owner is of record; and

(B) has priority over any conflicting interest of a predecessor in title of the encumbrancer or owner.

2) before the goods become fixtures, the security interest is perfected by any method permitted by this article, and the fixtures are readily removable:

(A) factory or office machines;

(B) equipment that is not primarily used or leased for use in the operation of the real property; or

(C) replacements of domestic consumer appliances.

3) the conflicting interest is a lien on the real property obtained by legal or equitable proceedings after a method permitted by this article perfected the security interest; or

4) the security interest is created in a manufactured home in a manufactured-home transaction; and

Priority based on consent, disclaimer, or right to remove

A security interest in fixtures, whether or not perfected, has priority over a conflicting interest of an encumbrancer or owner of the real property if:

1) the encumbrancer has, in an authenticated record, consented to the security interest or disclaimed it in the goods as fixtures; or

2) the debtor has a right to remove the goods as against the encumbrancer or owner.

The priority of the security interest continues for a reasonable time if the debtor's right to remove the goods as against the encumbrancer or owner terminates.

Priority of construction mortgage

A mortgage is a construction mortgage to the extent that it secures an obligation incurred to construct an improvement on land, including the acquisition cost of the land if a recorded record of the mortgage so indicates.

Except as otherwise provided, a security interest in fixtures is subordinate to a construction mortgage if a record of the mortgage is recorded before the goods become fixtures and the goods become fixtures before the completion of the construction.

A mortgage has this priority to the same extent as a construction mortgage to the extent that it is given to refinance a construction mortgage.

Priority of security interest in crops

A perfected security interest in crops growing on real property has priority over a conflicting interest of an encumbrancer or owner of the real property if the debtor has an interest of record in or is in possession of the real property.

§ 9-335. Accessions

Accession means goods physically united with other goods so that the identity of the original goods is *not* lost.

Creation of security interest in an accession

A security interest may be created in an accession and continues in collateral as an accession.

Perfection of security interest

If a security interest is perfected when the collateral becomes an accession, the security interest remains perfected in the collateral.

Priority of security interest

Except as otherwise provided, the other provisions of this part determine the priority of a security interest in an accession.

Compliance with the certificate-of-title statute

A security interest in an accession is subordinate to a security interest in the whole, perfected by compliance with the requirements of a certificate-of-title statute.

Removal of accession after default

After default, a secured party may remove an accession from other goods if the security interest in the accession has priority over the claims of every person having an interest in the whole.

Reimbursement following removal

A secured party that removes an accession from other goods shall promptly reimburse any holder of a security interest in, or owner of, the whole or of the other goods, other than the debtor, for the cost of repair of physical injury to the whole or the other goods.

The secured party need not reimburse the holder or owner for diminution in value of the whole or the other goods caused by the absence of the accession removed or by any necessity for replacing it.

A person entitled to reimbursement may refuse permission to remove until the secured party gives adequate assurance for the performance of the obligation to reimburse.

§ 9-336. Commingled Goods

"Commingled goods" means goods physically united with other goods, so their identity is lost in a product or mass.

No security interest in commingled goods as such

A security interest does not exist in commingled goods as such.

A security interest may attach to a product or mass that results when goods become commingled goods.

Attachment of security interest to product or mass

If collateral becomes commingled, a security interest attaches to the product.

Perfection of security interest

If a security interest in collateral is perfected before the collateral becomes commingled, the security interest attached to the product is perfected.

Priority of security interest

Except as otherwise provided, the other provisions of this part determine the priority of a security interest that attaches to the product.

Conflicting security interests in product or mass

If more than one security interest attaches to the product or mass under subsection (c), the following rules determine priority:

1) A perfected security interest has priority over a security interest that is unperfected when the collateral becomes commingled goods.

2) If more than one security interest is perfected, the security interests rank equally in proportion to the value of the collateral at the time it became commingled goods.

§ 9-339. Priority Subject to Subordination

This article does not preclude subordination by agreement by a person entitled to priority.

Rights of Third Parties

§ 9-401. Alienability of Debtor's Rights

Whether a debtor's rights in collateral may be voluntarily or involuntarily transferred is governed by a law other than this article.

An agreement does not prevent the transfer

An agreement between the debtor and secured party, which prohibits a transfer of the debtor's rights in collateral or makes the transfer a default, does not prevent transfer.

§ 9-404. Rights Acquired by Assignee; Claims And Defenses Against Assignee

Assignee's rights subject to terms, claims, and defenses; exceptions

Unless an account debtor has made an enforceable agreement not to assert defenses or claims, the rights of an assignee are subject to:

1) terms of the agreement between the account debtor and assignor and any defense or claim in recoupment arising from the transaction that gave rise to the contract; and

2) the defense or claim of the account debtor against the assignor accrues before the account debtor receives a notification of the assignment authenticated by the assignor or the assignee.

Account debtor's claim reduces the amount owed to an assignee

The claim of an account debtor against an assignor may be asserted against an assignee only to reduce the amount the account debtor owes.

Rule for individual under other law

This section is subject to law other than this article which establishes a different rule for an account debtor who is an individual and who incurred the obligation primarily for personal, family, or household purposes.

Omission of the required statement in a consumer transaction

In a consumer transaction, if a record evidences the account debtor's obligation, and the law requires that the record include a statement about the account debtor's recovery against an assignee for claims and defenses against the assignor may not exceed amounts paid by the debtor, and the record does not include such a statement, the extent that a debtor against the assignor is determined as if the record included such a statement.

Inapplicability to healthcare insurance receivables

This does not apply to an assignment of a health-care-insurance receivable.

§ 9-405. Modification of Assigned Contract

Effect of modification on the assignee

A modification of or substitution for an assigned contract is effective against an assignee if made in good faith.

The assignee acquires corresponding rights under the modified or substituted contract.

The assignment may provide that the modification or substitution is a breach of contract by the assignor.

Applicability of subsection above

Subsection above applies to the extent that:

1) the right to payment or a part thereof under an assigned contract has not been fully earned by performance; or

2) the right to payment has been fully earned by performance, and the account debtor has not received notification of the assignment.

Rules for individuals under other law

This section is subject to law other than this article which establishes a different rule for an account debtor who is an individual and who incurred the obligation primarily for personal, family, or household purposes.

§ 9-406. Account Debtor Discharge; Notification; Restrictions on Assignment

Discharge of account debtor; effect of notification

An account debtor on an account, chattel paper, or payment may discharge its obligation by paying the assignor until, but not after, the debtor receives notification, authenticated by the assignor or the assignee, that the amount due has been assigned and that payment is to be made to the assignee.

After receiving notification, the account debtor may discharge its obligation by paying the assignee and may not discharge the obligation by paying the assignor.

When notification ineffective

Notification is ineffective:

1) if it does not reasonably identify the rights assigned;

2) to the extent that an agreement between an account debtor and a seller of an intangible payment limits the debtor's duty to pay other than the seller and the limitation is effective under the law; or

3) at the option of an account debtor, if the notification notifies the account debtor to make less than the full amount of installment or periodic payment to the assignee, even if:

(A) only a portion of the account, chattel paper, or payment intangible has been assigned to that assignee;

(B) a portion has been assigned to another assignee; or

(C) the account debtor knows that the assignment to that assignee is limited.

Proof of assignment

If requested by the account debtor, an assignee shall seasonably furnish reasonable proof that the assignment has been made.

Unless the assignee complies, the account debtor may discharge its obligation by paying the assignor, even if the account debtor has received a notification.

Term restricting assignment generally ineffective

A term in an agreement between an account debtor and an assignor or a promissory note is ineffective to the extent that it:

1) prohibits, restricts, or requires the consent of the account debtor obligated on the promissory note to the assignment or transfer of, or the creation, perfection, or enforcement of a security interest in, the account, chattel paper, payment intangible, or promissory note; or

2) provides that the assignment or transfer or the creation, attachment, perfection, or enforcement of the security interest may give rise to a default, breach, right of recoupment, claim, defense, termination, right of termination, or remedy under the account, chattel paper, payment intangible, or promissory note.

Legal restrictions on assignments were generally ineffective

A rule of law, statute, or regulation that prohibits, restricts, or requires the consent of a government, or official, or account debtor to the assignment or transfer of, or creation of a security interest in, an account or chattel paper is ineffective to the extent that the rule of law, statute, or regulation:

1) prohibits, restricts, or requires the consent of the government, governmental body or official, or account debtor to the assignment or transfer of, or the creation, attachment, perfection, or enforcement of a security interest in the account or chattel paper; or

2) provides that the creation, attachment, perfection, or enforcement of the security interest may give rise to a default, breach, right of recoupment, claim, defense, termination, right of termination, or remedy under the account or chattel paper.

Subsection (b)(3) not waivable

Except as otherwise provided, an account debtor may not waive or vary its option.

Rules for individuals under other law

This section is subject to law other than this article which establishes a different rule for an account debtor who is an individual and who incurred the obligation primarily for personal, family, or household purposes.

Inapplicability to healthcare insurance receivables

This section does not apply to an assignment of a healthcare insurance receivable.

Filing Office – Contents and Effectiveness of Financing Statement

§ 9-501. Filing Office

If the law of the State governs perfection of a security interest or agricultural lien, the office in which to file a financing statement to perfect the security interest or agricultural lien is:

1) the office designated for the filing or recording of a record of a mortgage on the related real property, if:

(A) the collateral is as-extracted or timber to be cut; or

(B) the financing statement is filed as a fixture filing, and the collateral is goods that are or are to become fixtures; or

2) the office duly authorized, in all other cases, including a case in which the collateral is goods that are or are to become fixtures, and the financing statement, is not filed as a fixture filing.

Filing office for transmitting utilities

The office in which to file a financing statement to perfect a security interest in collateral, including fixtures, of a transmitting utility, is the [state designated office].

The financing statement constitutes a fixture filing as to the collateral indicated in the financing statement, which is or is to become fixtures.

§ 9-512. Amendment of Financing Statement

Alternative A: Amendment of information in the financing statements

A person may add or delete collateral, continue, or terminate the effectiveness of, or otherwise amend the information provided in, a financing statement by filing an amendment that:

1) identifies, by its file number, the initial financing statement to which the amendment relates; and

2) if the amendment relates to an initial financing statement filed [or recorded] in a filing office.

Alternative B: Period of effectiveness not affected

The filing of an amendment does not extend the period for the financing statement.

Effectiveness of amendment adding collateral

A financing statement that is amended by an amendment adding collateral is effective as to the added collateral from the date of the filing of the amendment.

Effectiveness of amendment adding debtor

A financing statement that is amended by an amendment that adds a debtor is effective as to the added debtor only from the date of the filing of the amendment.

Certain amendments ineffective

An amendment is ineffective to the extent it:

1) purports to delete all debtors and fails to provide the name of a debtor to be covered by the financing statement; or

2) purports to delete all secured parties of record and fails to provide the name of a new secured party of record.

§ 9-513. Termination Statement

Consumer goods

A secured party shall cause the secured party of record for a financing statement to file a termination statement for the financing statement if the financing statement covers consumer goods and:

1) there is no obligation secured by the collateral covered by the financing statement and no commitment to advance, incur an obligation, or otherwise give value; or

2) the debtor did not authorize the filing of the initial financing statement.

Time for compliance

A secured party shall cause the secured party of record to file the termination statement:

1) within one month after there is no obligation secured by the collateral covered by the financing statement and no commitment to make an advance, incur an obligation, or otherwise give value; or

2) if earlier, within 20 days after the secured party receives an authenticated demand from a debtor.

Other collateral

Within 20 days after a secured party receives an authenticated demand from a debtor, the secured party shall cause the secured party of record for a financing statement to send the debtor a termination statement for the financing statement or file the termination statement in the filing office if:

> 1) except in the case of a financing statement covering accounts or chattel paper that has been sold or goods the subject of a consignment, there is no obligation secured by the collateral covered by the financing statement and no commitment to make an advance, incur an obligation, or otherwise give value;

> 2) the financing statement covers accounts or chattel paper that has been sold, but the account debtor or another person obligated has discharged their obligation;

> 3) the financing statement covers goods that were the subject of a consignment to the debtor but are not in the debtor's possession; or

> 4) the debtor did not authorize the filing of the financing statement.

Effect of filing termination statement

Upon filing a termination statement with the filing office, the financing statement to which the termination statement relates ceases to be effective.

The filing with the filing office of a termination statement relating to a financing statement indicates that the debtor is a transmitting utility and causes the financing statement's effectiveness to lapse.

§ 9-514. Assignment of Powers of Secured Party of Record

Assignment reflected on the initial financing statement

An initial financing statement may reflect an assignment of the secured party's power to authorize an amendment to the financing statement by providing the name and mailing address of the assignee as the name and address of the secured party.

Assignment of the filed financing statement

A secured party of record may assign of record all or part of its power to authorize an amendment to a financing statement by filing in the filing office an amendment of the financing statement which:

1) identifies, by its file number, the initial financing statement;

2) provides the name of the assignor; and

3) provides the name and mailing address of the assignee.

Assignment of record of mortgage

An assignment of record of a security interest in a fixture covered by a record of a mortgage which is effective as a financing statement filed as a fixture filing, may be made only by an assignment of record of the mortgage as provided by law.

§ 9-519. Maintaining Records; Communicating Record's Information

Filing office duties

For each record filed in a filing office, the filing office shall:

1) assign a unique number to the filed record;

2) create a record that bears the number with date and time of filing;

3) maintain the filed record for public inspection; and

4) index the filed record following subsections (c), (d), and (e).

File number

A file number [assigned after January 1, 2002,] must include a digit that:

1) is mathematically derived from the digits of the file number; and

2) aids the filing office in determining whether the file number includes a single-digit or transpositional error.

Indexing: general

The filing office shall:

1) index an initial financing statement by the name of the debtor and index filed records relating to the initial financing statement in a manner that associates with one another an initial financing statement and filed records relating to the initial financing statement; and

2) index a record that provides a name of a debtor which was not previously provided in the financing statement to which the record also relates according to the name that was not previously provided.

Indexing: real-property-related financing statement

If a financing statement is filed as a fixture filing or covers as-extracted collateral or timber to be cut, the filing office shall index it:

1) under the names of the debtor and of each owner of record shown on the financing statement as if they were the mortgagors under a mortgage of the real property described; and

2) to the extent that the law of this State provides for indexing of records of mortgages under the name of the mortgagee, under the name of the secured party as if the secured party were the mortgagee thereunder, or if indexing is by description as if the financing statement were a record of a mortgage of the real property described.

Indexing: real-property-related assignments

If a financing statement is filed as a fixture filing or covers as-extracted collateral or timber to be cut, the filing office shall index an assignment filed:

1) under the name of the assignor as grantor; and

2) to the extent that the State law provides for indexing a record of the assignment of a mortgage under the name of the assignee.

Alternative A: Retrieval and association capability

The filing office shall maintain a capability:

> 1) to retrieve a record by the name of the debtor and by the file number assigned to the initial financing statement to which the record relates; and

> 2) to associate and retrieve an initial financing statement and each filed record relating to the initial financing statement.

Alternative B: Retrieval and association capability

The filing office shall maintain a capability:

> 1) to retrieve a record by the name of the debtor and:

>> (A) if the filing office is described in Section 9-501(a)(1), by the file number assigned to the initial financing statement to which the record relates and the date [and time] that the record was filed [or recorded]; or

>> (B) if the filing office is described in Section 9-501(a)(2), by the file number assigned to the initial financing statement to which the record relates; and

> 2) to associate and retrieve an initial financing statement and each filed record relating to the initial financing statement.

[End of Alternatives]

Removal of debtor's name

The filing office may not remove a debtor's name from the index until one year after the effectiveness of a financing statement naming the debtor lapses for secured parties of record.

Timeliness of filing office performance

The filing office shall perform the acts required at the time and in the manner prescribed by the filing-office rule, but not later than two business days after the filing office receives the record in question.

Default and Enforcement of Security Interest

§ 9-601. Rights After Default; Judicial Enforcement

Rights of secured party after default

After default, a secured party has the rights provided in this part and, except as otherwise provided by the agreement of the parties.

A secured party:

> 1) may reduce a claim to judgment, or enforce the claim, security interest, or agricultural lien by available judicial procedure; and

> 2) if the collateral documents may proceed as to documents or goods they cover.

Rights and duties of the secured party in possession or control

A secured party in possession of collateral has the rights and duties.

Rights cumulative; simultaneous exercise

The rights are cumulative and may be exercised simultaneously.

Rights of debtor and obligor

Except as otherwise provided, after default, a debtor and an obligor have the rights provided in this part and by agreement of the parties.

Lien of levy after judgment

If a secured party has reduced its claim to judgment, the lien of any levy that may be made upon the collateral by an execution based upon the judgment relates to the earliest of:

> 1) the date of perfection of the security interest or agricultural lien in the collateral;

> 2) the date of filing a financing statement covering the collateral; or

> 3) any date specified in a statute under which the agricultural lien was created.

Execution sale

A sale according to an execution is a foreclosure of the security interest or agricultural lien by judicial procedure within the meaning of this section.

A secured party may purchase at the sale and thereafter hold the collateral free of other requirements of this article.

Consignor or buyer of certain rights to payment

This part imposes no duties upon a secured party that is a consignor or is a buyer of accounts, chattel paper, payment intangibles, or promissory notes.

§ 9-602. Waiver and Variance of Rights and Duties

To the extent that they give rights to a debtor or obligor and impose duties on a secured party, the debtor or obligor may not waive or vary the rules stated in the following listed sections:

1) use and operation of the collateral by the secured party;

2) requests for an accounting concerning a list of collateral and statement of account;

3) collection and enforcement of collateral;

4) application or payment of noncash proceeds, enforcement, or disposition;

5) require accounting for or payment of proceeds of collateral;

6) imposes upon a secured party that takes possession of collateral without judicial process the duty not to breach the peace;

7) the disposition of collateral;

8) calculation of a deficiency or surplus when a disposition is made to the secured party, a person related to the secured party, or a secondary obligor;

9) explanation of the calculation of a surplus or deficiency;

10) acceptance of collateral in satisfaction of obligation;

11) the redemption of collateral;

12) permissible waivers; and

13) the secured party's liability for failure to comply with this article.

§ 9-603. Agreed Standards Concerning Rights and Duties

The parties may determine by agreement the standards measuring the fulfillment of the rights of a debtor or obligor and the duties of a secured party if the standards are not manifestly unreasonable.

Agreed standards inapplicable to breach of peace.

§ 9-604. Procedure from Real Property or Fixtures

Personal and real property enforcement

If a security agreement covers personal and real property, a secured party may proceed:

> 1) under this part as to the personal property without prejudicing any rights to the real property; or

> 2) as to personal property and real property per the rights to real property, the other provisions of this part do not apply.

Enforcement for fixtures

Subject to subsection (c), if a security agreement covers goods that are or become fixtures, a secured party may proceed:

> 1) under this part; or

> 2) per the rights to real property, the other provisions of this part do not apply.

Removal of fixtures

If a secured party holding a security interest in fixtures has priority over owners and encumbrancers of the real property, the secured party, after default, may remove the collateral from the real property.

Injury caused by removal

A secured party that removes collateral shall promptly reimburse any encumbrancer or owner of the real property, other than the debtor, for the cost of repair of physical injury caused by the removal.

The secured party need not reimburse the encumbrancer or owner for diminution in value of the real property caused by the absence of the goods removed or by necessity of replacing them.

A person entitled to reimbursement may refuse permission to remove until the secured party gives adequate assurance for the performance of the obligation to reimburse.

§ 9-605. Unknown Debtor or Secondary Obligor

A secured party does not owe a duty based on status as a secured party:

> 1) to a person that is a debtor, unless the secured party knows:
>
>> (A) that the person is a debtor or obligor;
>>
>> (B) the identity of the person; and
>>
>> (C) how to communicate with the person; or
>
> 2) to a secured party or lienholder that has filed a financing statement against a person unless the secured party knows:
>
>> (A) that the person is a debtor; and
>>
>> (B) the identity of the person.

§ 9-606. Time of Default for Agricultural Lien

A default occurs with an agricultural lien when the secured party becomes entitled to enforce the lien under the statute.

§ 9-607. Collection and Enforcement by Secured Party

Collection and enforcement generally

If so agreed, and in any event after default, a secured party:

> 1) may notify an account debtor or other person obligated on collateral to make a payment or otherwise render performance to or for the benefit of the secured party;
>
> 2) may take proceeds to which the secured party is entitled;
>
> 3) may enforce the obligations of an account debtor or other person obligated on collateral and exercise the rights of the debtor to the obligation of the account debtor or other person obligated on collateral to make the payment or render performance to the debtor, and to property that secures the obligations of the account debtor or other person obligated on the collateral;
>
> 4) if it holds a security interest in a deposit account perfected by control under, may apply the balance of the deposit account to the obligation secured by the deposit account; and
>
> 5) if it holds a security interest in a deposit account perfected by control, may instruct the bank to pay the balance of the account to or for the benefit of the secured party.

Nonjudicial enforcement of mortgage

If necessary to enable a secured party to exercise the right of a debtor to enforce a mortgage nonjudicially, the secured party may record in the office in which a record of the mortgage is recorded:

1) a copy of the security agreement that provides for a security interest in the obligation secured by the mortgage; and

2) the secured party's affidavit in recordable form stating that:

(A) a default has occurred for the obligation secured by the mortgage; and

(B) the secured party is entitled to enforce the mortgage nonjudicially.

Commercially reasonable collection and enforcement

A secured party shall proceed in a commercially reasonable manner if the secured party:

1) undertakes to collect from or enforce an obligation of an account debtor or other person obligated on collateral; and

2) is entitled to charge back uncollected collateral or otherwise to full or limited recourse against the debtor or a secondary obligor.

Expenses of collection and enforcement

A secured party may deduct from the collection's reasonable expenses of collection and enforcement, including reasonable attorney's fees and legal expenses incurred by the secured party.

Duties to the secured party not affected

This section does not determine whether an account debtor, bank, or other person obligated on collateral owes a duty to a secured party.

§ 9-608. Liability for Deficiency and Right to Surplus

Application of proceeds, surplus and deficiency

If a security interest or agricultural lien secures payment or performance of an obligation, the following rules apply:

1) A secured party shall apply or pay over for application the cash proceeds of collection or enforcement in the following order to:

(A) the reasonable expenses of collection and enforcement and, to the extent provided for by agreement and not prohibited by law, reasonable attorney's fees and legal expenses incurred by the secured party;

(B) the satisfaction of obligations secured by the security interest or agricultural lien under which the collection or enforcement is made; and

(C) the satisfaction of obligations secured by any subordinate security interest in the collateral subject to the security interest or agricultural lien under which the collection or enforcement is made if the secured party receives an authenticated demand for proceeds before distribution of the proceeds is completed.

2) If requested by a secured party, a holder of a subordinate security interest shall furnish reasonable proof of the interest or lien within a reasonable time.

Unless the holder complies, the secured party need not comply with the holder's demand under paragraph (1)(C).

3) A secured party need not apply or pay over for noncash proceeds of collection and enforcement unless the failure to do so would be commercially unreasonable.

A secured party that applies or pays over for application noncash proceeds shall do so in a commercially reasonable manner.

4) A secured party shall account to and pay a debtor for surplus, and the obligor is liable for the deficiency.

No surplus or deficiency in sales of certain rights to payment

If the underlying transaction is a sale of accounts, chattel paper, payment intangibles, or promissory notes, the debtor is not entitled to surplus, and the obligor is not liable for the deficiency.

§ 9-609. Secured Party's Right to Possession After Default

Possession; rendering equipment unusable; disposition on debtor's premises

After default, a secured party:

> 1) may take possession of the collateral; and

> 2) without removal, may render equipment unusable and dispose of collateral on a debtor's premises.

Judicial and nonjudicial process

A secured party may proceed:

> 1) according to judicial process; or

> 2) without judicial process, without breach of the peace.

Assembly of collateral

If so agreed, and in any event after default, a secured party may require the debtor to assemble the collateral and make it available to the secured party at a place to be designated by the secured party, which is reasonably convenient to each party.

§ 9-610. Disposition of Collateral After Default

Disposition after default

After default, a secured party may sell, lease, license, or otherwise dispose of the collateral in its present condition or following commercially reasonable preparation or processing.

Commercially reasonable disposition

Every aspect of a disposition of collateral, including the method, manner, time, place, and other terms, must be commercially reasonable.

If commercially reasonable, a secured party may dispose of collateral by public or private proceedings, by one or more contracts, as a unit or in parcels, and at any time and place and on any terms.

Purchase by the secured party

A secured party may purchase collateral:

> 1) at a public disposition; or

> 2) at a private disposition only if the collateral is customarily sold on a recognized market or the subject of standard price quotations.

Warranties on disposition

A contract for sale, lease, license, or other disposition includes the warranties relating to title, possession, and quiet enjoyment, which accompany a voluntary disposition of property of the kind subject to the contract.

Disclaimer of warranties

A secured party may disclaim or modify warranties under subsection (d):

> 1) in a manner that would be effective to disclaim or modify the warranties in a voluntary disposition of property of the kind subject to the contract of disposition; or

> 2) by communicating to the purchaser a record evidencing the contract for disposition and including an express disclaimer or modification of the warranties.

Record sufficient to disclaim warranties

A record is enough to disclaim warranties if it indicates "There is no warranty relating to title, possession, quiet enjoyment, or the like in this disposition" or uses words of similar import.

§ 9-611. Notification Before Disposition of Collateral

Notification date means the earlier of the date on which:

> 1) a secured party sends to the debtor and any secondary obligor an authenticated notification of disposition; or

> 2) the debtor and any secondary obligor waive the right to notification.

Notification of disposition required

A secured party that disposes of collateral shall send to the persons specified a reasonable authenticated notification of disposition.

Persons to be notified

To comply, the secured party shall send notification of disposition to:

1) the debtor;

2) any secondary obligor; and

3) if the collateral is other than consumer goods:

(A) any person from which the secured party has received, before the notification date, an authenticated notification of a claim of an interest in the collateral;

(B) any other secured party or lienholder that, 10 days before the notification date, held a security interest perfected by the filing of a financing statement that:

(i) identified the collateral;

(ii) was indexed under the debtor's name as of that date; and

(iii) was filed in the office in which to file a financing statement against the debtor covering the collateral as of that date; and

(C) another secured party that, 10 days before the notification date, held a security interest in the collateral perfected by compliance with a statute, regulation, or treaty.

Subsection inapplicable: perishable collateral; recognized market

Subsection does not apply if the collateral is perishable or threatens to decline speedily in value or is of a type customarily sold on a recognized market.

Compliance with subsection (c)(3)(B)

A secured party complies with the requirement for notification prescribed:

1) not later than 20 or earlier than 30 days before the notification date, the secured party requests, in a commercially reasonable manner, information concerning financing statements indexed under the debtor's name in the office indicated; and

2) before the notification date, the secured party:

(A) did not receive a response to the request for information; or

(B) received a response to the request for information and sent an authenticated notification of disposition to each secured party or other lienholder named in that response whose financing statement covered the collateral.

§ 9-612. Notification Timeliness Before Disposition of Collateral

Reasonable time is a question of fact

Whether notification is sent within a reasonable time is a question of fact.

10-day period sufficient in non-consumer transactions

In a transaction other than a consumer transaction, a notification of disposition is sent after default and ten days or more before the earliest time of disposition outlined in the notification is sent within a reasonable time before the disposition.

§ 9-613. Notification Form and Content Before Disposition of Collateral

The following rules apply:

1) A notification of disposition is enough if the notification:

   (A) describes the debtor and the secured party;

   (B) describes the collateral subject to the disposition;

   (C) states the method of intended disposition;

   (D) states that debtor is entitled to an accounting of the indebtedness and states the charge for an accounting; and

   (E) states the time and place of a public disposition or the time after which any other disposition is to be made.

2) Whether the contents of a notification that lacks any of the information specified are nevertheless enough a question of fact.

3) The contents of a notification providing substantially the information specified in paragraph (1) are sufficient, even if the notification includes: (A) information not specified by that paragraph; or (B) minor errors that are not seriously misleading.

4) A particular phrasing of the notification is not required.

5) The following form of notification and the form appearing in Section 9-614(3) each provides enough information:

SAMPLE

NOTIFICATION OF DISPOSITION OF COLLATERAL

To: [Name of debtor or obligor]

From: [Name, address, and telephone number of the secured party]

Name of Debtor(s): [Include only if debtor(s) are not an addressee]

[For a public disposition:]

We will sell [or lease or license] the [describe collateral] to the highest qualified bidder in public as follows:

Day and Date: _________   Time: _________   Place: _________

[For a private disposition:]

We will sell [or lease or license] the [describe collateral] privately sometime after [day and date].

You are entitled to an accounting of the unpaid indebtedness secured by the property that we intend to dispose of for a charge of $ ____.

You may request an accounting by calling us.

[End of Form]

§ 9-614. Notification Before Disposition: Consumer-Goods Transactions

In a consumer-goods transaction, the following rules apply:

1) A notification of disposition must provide the following:

(A) the information specified in Section 9-613(1);

(B) a description of liability for a deficiency of the person to which the notification is sent;

(C) a telephone number for which the amount that must be paid to the secured party to redeem the collateral; and

(D) a telephone number or mailing address for information about the disposition and the obligation secured is available.

2) A particular phrasing of the notification is not required.

3) The following form of notification, when completed, provides enough information:

SAMPLE

NOTICE OF OUR PLAN TO SELL PROPERTY

[Name and address of secured party]   [Date]

[Name and address of obligor who is also a debtor]

Subject: [Identification of Transaction]

We have your [collateral] because you broke promises in our agreement.

[For a public disposition:]

We will dispose of [describe collateral] at public sale.

The sale will be held as follows:

Date: _____   Time: _____   Place: _____

You may attend the sale and bring bidders if you want.

[For a private disposition:]

We will sell dispose of [describe collateral] at a private sale after [date].

The money that we get from the sale (after paying our costs) will reduce the amount you owe. If we get less money than owed, you may still owe the difference. If we get more money than you owe, you will get the extra money unless we must pay it to someone else.

You can get the property back at any time before we sell it by paying us the full amount you owe (not just the past due payments), including our expenses. To learn the exact amount you must pay, call us at [telephone number].

If you want us to explain to you in writing how we have figured the amount owed us, you may call us at [number] or write us at [secured party's address] and request a written explanation. We charge $ 50 for the explanation if we sent another explanation within the last six months.

If you need more information about the sale, call us at [telephone number] or write to us at [secured party's address].

We are sending this notice to the following other people who have an interest in [describe collateral] or who owe money under your agreement:

[Names of other debtors and obligors, if any]

[End of form]

§ 9-615. Proceeds; Liability for Deficiency and Right to Surplus

Application of proceeds

A secured party shall apply or pay over for application the cash proceeds of disposition in the following order to:

> 1) the reasonable expenses of retaking, holding, preparing for disposition, processing, and disposing of, and, to the extent provided for by agreement and not prohibited by law, reasonable attorney's fees and legal expenses incurred by the secured party;

> 2) the satisfaction of obligations secured by the security interest or agricultural lien under which the disposition is made;

> 3) the satisfaction of obligations secured by a subordinate security interest in or another subordinate lien on the collateral if:

>> (A) the secured party receives from the holder of the subordinate security interest a demand for proceeds before distribution of the proceeds is completed; and

>> (B) in a case in which a consignor has an interest in the collateral, the subordinate security interest is senior to the interest of the consignor; and

> 4) a secured party that is a consignor of the collateral if the secured party receives from the consignor an authenticated demand for proceeds before distribution of the proceeds is completed.

Proof of subordinate interest

If requested by a secured party, a holder of a subordinate security interest shall furnish reasonable proof of the interest or lien within a reasonable time.

Application of noncash proceeds

A secured party need not apply or pay the noncash proceeds of disposition unless the failure to do so would be commercially unreasonable.

A secured party that applies or pays over for application noncash proceeds shall do so in a commercially reasonable manner.

Surplus or deficiency if obligation secured

If the security interest under which a disposition is made secures payment or performance of an obligation, after making the payments:

> 1) the secured party shall pay a debtor for surplus; and

> 2) the obligor is liable for deficiency.

No surplus or deficiency in sales of certain rights to payment

If the underlying transaction is a sale of accounts, chattel paper, payment intangibles, or promissory notes:

> 1) the debtor is not entitled to surplus; and

> 2) the obligor is not liable for deficiency.

Surplus or deficiency in disposition to a person related to the secured party

The surplus or deficiency following disposition is calculated based on the proceeds that would have been realized in a disposition complying with this part to a transferee other than the secured party, a person related to the secured party, or a secondary obligor if:

> 1) the transferee in the disposition is the secured party, a person related to the secured party, or a secondary obligor; and

> 2) the amount of proceeds of the disposition is significantly below the range of proceeds that a complying disposition to a person other than the secured party, a person related to the secured party, or a secondary obligor would have brought.

Cash proceeds received by the junior secured party

A secured party that receives cash proceeds of a disposition in good faith and without knowledge that the receipt violates the rights of the holder of a security interest that is not subordinate to the security interest or agricultural lien under which the disposition is made:

> 1) takes the cash proceeds free of the security interest or other liens;

> 2) is not obligated to apply the proceeds of the disposition to the satisfaction of obligations secured by the security interest; and

> 3) is not obligated to pay the holder of the security for surplus.

§ 9-616. Calculation of Surplus or Deficiency

Explanation means a writing that:

(A) states the amount of the surplus or deficiency;

(B) how the secured party calculated the surplus or deficiency;

(C) states that future debits, credits, charges, including additional credit service charges or interest, and expenses may affect the amount of the surplus or deficiency; and

(D) provides a telephone number or mailing address from which additional information concerning the transaction is available.

Request means a record:

(A) authenticated by a debtor or consumer obligor;

(B) requesting that the recipient explain; and

(C) sent after disposition of the collateral.

Explanation of calculations

In a consumer-goods transaction in which the debtor is entitled to a surplus or a consumer obligor is liable for a deficiency, the secured party shall:

1) send an explanation to the debtor or consumer obligor, as applicable, after the disposition and:

(A) before or when the secured party accounts to the debtor and pays surplus or first makes written demand on the consumer obligor after the disposition for payment of the deficiency; and

(B) within 14 days after receipt of a request; or

2) in the case of a consumer obligor who is liable for a deficiency, within 14 days after receipt of a request, send to the consumer obligor a record waiving the secured party's right to a deficiency.

Required information

To comply, a writing must provide the information in the following order:

1) the aggregate amount of obligations secured by the security interest under which the disposition was made, and, if the amount reflects a rebate of unearned interest or credit service charge, an indication of that fact, calculated as of a specified date:

(A) if the secured party takes or receives possession of the collateral after default, not more than 35 days before the secured party takes or receives possession; or

(B) if the secured party takes or receives possession of the collateral before default or does not take possession of the collateral, not more than 35 days before the disposition;

2) the amount of proceeds of the disposition;

3) the aggregate amount of the obligations after deducting proceeds;

4) the amount, in the aggregate or by type, and types of expenses, including expenses of retaking, holding, preparing for disposition, processing, and disposing of the collateral, and attorney's fees secured by the collateral which is known to the secured party and relates to the current disposition;

5) the amount and types of credits, including interest or credit service charges, to which the obligor is entitled; and

6) the amount of the surplus or deficiency.

Substantial compliance

A particular phrasing of the explanation is not required.

An explanation complying substantially with the requirements, even if it includes minor errors that are not seriously misleading.

Charges for responses

A debtor or consumer obligor is entitled without charge to one response to a request under this section during any six-month period in which the secured party did not send to the debtor or consumer obligor an explanation.

The secured party may require payment of a charge not exceeding $25 for each additional response.

§ 9-617. Rights of Transferee of Collateral

Effects of disposition

A secured party's disposition of collateral after default:

> 1) transfers to a transferee for value all of the debtor's rights in the collateral;
>
> 2) discharges the security interest; and
>
> 3) discharges subordinate security interests or subordinate liens.

Rights of good-faith transferee

A transferee that acts in good faith takes free of the rights and interests, even if the secured party fails to comply with this article or the requirements of any judicial proceeding.

Rights of another transferee

If a transferee does not take free of the rights and interests, the transferee takes the collateral subject to:

> 1) the debtor's rights in the collateral;
>
> 2) the security interest or agricultural lien under which the disposition is made; and
>
> 3) any other security interest.

§ 9-618. Rights and Duties of Certain Secondary Obligors

A secondary obligor acquires the rights and becomes obligated to perform the duties of the secured party after the secondary obligor:

> 1) receives an assignment of secured obligation from the secured party;
>
> 2) receives a transfer of collateral from the secured party and agrees to accept the rights and assume the duties of the secured party; or
>
> 3) is subrogated to the rights of a secured party for the collateral.

Effect of assignment, transfer, or subrogation

An assignment, transfer, or subrogation described in subsection (a):

> 1) is not a disposition of collateral; and
>
> 2) relieves the secured party of further duties under this article.

§ 9-619. Transfer of Record or Legal Title

Transfer statement means a record authenticated by a secured party stating:

1) the debtor has defaulted in connection with an obligation secured by specified collateral;

2) the secured party has exercised its post-default remedies concerning the collateral;

3) that, because of the exercise, a transferee has acquired the rights of the debtor in the collateral; and

4) the name and address of the secured party, debtor, and transferee.

Effect of transfer statement

A transfer statement entitles the transferee to the transfer of record of all rights of the debtor in the collateral specified in the statement in any official filing, recording, registration, or certificate-of-title system covering the collateral.

If a transfer statement is presented with the applicable fee and request form to the official or office responsible for maintaining the system, the office shall:

1) accept the transfer statement;

2) promptly amend its records to reflect the transfer; and

3) if applicable, issue a new appropriate certificate of title in the name of the transferee.

No relief of secured party's duties transfer without disposition

A transfer of the record or legal title to collateral to a secured party or otherwise is not of itself a disposition of collateral under this article and does not relieve the secured party of its duties under this article.

§ 9-620. Acceptance of Collateral in Satisfaction; Compulsory Disposition

Conditions to acceptance in satisfaction

A secured party may accept collateral in satisfaction of the obligation it secures only if:

1) the debtor consents to the acceptance;

2) the secured party does not receive a notification of objection to the proposal authenticated by:

> (A) a person to which the secured party was required to send a proposal; or

> (B) any other person, other than the debtor, holding an interest in the collateral subordinate to the security interest;

3) if the collateral is consumer goods, the collateral is not in possession of the debtor when the debtor accepts; and

4) subsection (e) does not require the secured party to dispose of the collateral, or the debtor waives the requirement.

Purported acceptance is ineffective

A purported acceptance of collateral under this section is ineffective unless:

1) the secured party consents to the acceptance in an authenticated record or sends a proposal to the debtor.

Debtor's consent

A debtor consents to an acceptance of collateral in partial satisfaction of the obligation it secures only if the debtor agrees to the terms of the acceptance in a record authenticated after default.

A debtor consents to an acceptance of collateral in satisfaction of the obligation it secures only if the debtor agrees to the terms of the acceptance in a record authenticated after default or the secured party:

> (A) sends to the debtor after default a proposal that is unconditional or subject only to a condition that collateral not in possession of the secured party be preserved or maintained;

> (B) in the proposal, proposes to accept collateral in satisfaction of the obligation it secures; and

> (C) does not receive a notification of objection authenticated by the debtor within 20 days after the proposal is sent.

Effectiveness of notification

Notification of objection must be received by the secured party:

1) in the case of a person to which the proposal was sent within 20 days after notification was sent to that person; and

2) in other cases: within 20 days of the last notification, or if a notification was not sent before the debtor consents to acceptance.

Mandatory disposition of consumer goods

A secured party that has taken possession of collateral shall dispose of the collateral within the time specified if:

1) 60 percent of the cash price has been paid in the case of a purchase-money security interest in consumer goods; or

2) 60 percent of the principal amount has been paid in the case of a non-purchase-money security interest in consumer goods.

Compliance with mandatory disposition requirement

The secured party shall dispose of the collateral:

1) within 90 days after taking possession; or

2) within any longer period to which the debtor and secondary obligors have agreed in an agreement to that effect entered and authenticated after default.

No partial satisfaction in a consumer transaction

A secured party may not accept collateral in a consumer transaction in partial satisfaction of the obligation it secures.

§ 9-621. Notification of Proposal to Accept Collateral

Persons to which proposal to be sent

A secured party that desires to accept collateral in full or partial satisfaction of the obligation it secures shall send its proposal to:

1) any person from which the secured party had received, before the debtor consented to the acceptance, an authenticated notification of a claim in the collateral;

2) any other secured party or lienholder that, ten days before the debtor consented to the acceptance, held a security interest in the collateral perfected by the filing of a financing statement that:

(A) identified the collateral;

(B) was indexed under the debtor's name as of that date; and

(C) was filed in the office in which to file a financing statement against the debtor covering the collateral as of that date; and

3) any other secured party that, 10 days before the debtor consented to the acceptance, held a security interest in the collateral perfected by compliance with a statute, regulation, or treaty.

Proposal to be sent to the secondary obligor in partial satisfaction

A secured party that desires to accept collateral in partial satisfaction of the obligation it secures shall send its proposal to any secondary obligor in addition to the persons described in subsection (a).

§ 9-622. Effect of Acceptance of Collateral

A secured party's acceptance of collateral in full or partial satisfaction of the obligation it secures:

1) discharges the obligation to the extent consented to by the debtor;

2) transfers to the secured party all debtor's rights in the collateral;

3) discharges the security interest or agricultural lien that is the subject of the debtor's consent and any subordinate security interest or another subordinate lien; and

4) terminates any other subordinate interest.

Discharge of subordinate interest, notwithstanding noncompliance

A subordinate interest is discharged or terminated, even if the secured party fails to comply with this article.

§ 9-623. Right to Redeem Collateral

Persons that may redeem

A debtor, secondary obligor, or other secured party or lienholder may redeem the collateral.

Requirements for redemption

To redeem the collateral, a person shall tender:

1) fulfillment of obligations secured by the collateral; and

2) the reasonable expenses and attorney's fees.

When redemption may occur

A redemption may occur at any time before a secured party:

1) has collected collateral;

2) has disposed of collateral; or

3) has accepted collateral in satisfaction of the obligation it secures.

§ 9-624. Waiver

Waiver of disposition notification

A debtor or secondary obligor may waive the right to notification of disposition of collateral only by an agreement to that effect entered and authenticated after default.

Waiver of mandatory disposition

A debtor may waive the right to require disposition of collateral only by an agreement to that effect entered and authenticated after default.

Waiver of redemption right

Except in a consumer-goods transaction, a debtor or secondary obligor may waive the right to redeem collateral only by an agreement to that effect entered and authenticated after default.

§ 9-625. Remedies for Secured Party's Failure Complying with Article

Judicial orders concerning noncompliance

If a secured party is not proceeding following this article, a court may order or restrain collection, enforcement, or disposition of collateral on appropriate terms and conditions.

Damages for noncompliance

A person is liable for damages caused by a failure to comply with this article.

Loss caused by a failure to comply may include loss resulting from the debtor's inability to obtain, or increased costs of, alternative financing.

Persons are entitled to recover statutory damages in a consumer-goods transaction.

At the time of failure, a debtor or holder of a security interest may recover damages.

If the collateral is consumer goods, a debtor or obligor when a secured party failed to comply may recover for that failure.

Recovery for an amount not less than the credit service charge plus 10 percent of the principal amount of the obligation or the time-price differential plus 10 percent of the cash price.

Recovery when deficiency eliminated or reduced

A debtor whose deficiency is eliminated may recover for the loss of surplus.

A debtor or secondary obligor whose deficiency is eliminated or reduced may not otherwise recover for noncompliance with the provisions of this part relating to the collection, enforcement, disposition, or acceptance.

Statutory damages: noncompliance with specified provisions.

In addition to damages recoverable, the debtor, consumer obligor, or person named as a debtor in a filed record, as applicable, may recover $500 in each case from a person that:

    1) fails to comply with Section 9-208, 9-209 and 9-616(b);

    2) files a record of no entitlement under Section 9-509(a);

    3) fails to cause the secured party of record to file or send a termination statement;

    4) fails to comply and whose failure is part of a pattern or consistent with a practice of noncompliance.

Statutory damages: noncompliance with Section 9-210

A debtor or consumer obligor may recover damages and $500 in each case from a person that, without reasonable cause, fails to comply with a request.

A recipient of a request which never claimed an interest in the collateral or obligations that are the subject of a request under that section has a reasonable excuse for failure to comply with the request within the meaning of this subsection.

Limitation of security interest: noncompliance with Section 9-210

If a secured party fails to comply with a request regarding a collateral list or a statement of account, the secured party may claim a security interest only as shown in the list or statement included in the request against a person reasonably misled by the failure.

§ 9-626. Deficiency or Surplus Is in Issue

Applicable rules if the amount of deficiency or surplus in an issue

In an action arising from a transaction, other than a consumer transaction, in which the amount of a deficiency or surplus is in issue, these rules apply:

1) A secured party need not prove compliance with the provisions of this part relating to the collection, enforcement, disposition, or acceptance unless the debtor or a secondary obligor places the secured party's compliance in the issue.

2) If the secured party's compliance is placed in issue, the secured party has the burden of establishing that the collection, enforcement, disposition, or acceptance was conducted following this part.

3) If a secured party fails to prove that the collection, enforcement, disposition, or acceptance was conducted per the provisions of this part relating to the collection, enforcement, disposition, or acceptance, the liability of a debtor or a secondary obligor for a deficiency is limited to an amount by which the sum of the secured obligation, expenses, and attorney's fees exceeds the greater of:

(A) the proceeds of the collection, enforcement, disposition, or acceptance; or

(B) the proceeds that would have been realized had the noncomplying secured party proceeded following the provisions of this part relating to the collection, enforcement, disposition, or acceptance.

4) The amount of proceeds that would have been realized is equal to the sum of the secured obligation, expenses, and attorney's fees unless the secured party proves that the amount is less than that sum.

5) If a deficiency or surplus is calculated, the debtor or obligor has the burden of establishing that the amount of proceeds of the disposition is significantly below the range of prices that a complying disposition to a person other than the secured party, a person related to the secured party, or a secondary obligor would have brought.

Non-consumer transactions with no inference

The limitation of the rules to transactions other than consumer transactions is intended to leave to the court the determination of the proper rules in consumer transactions.

The court may not infer from that limitation the nature of the proper rule in consumer transactions and may continue to apply established approaches.

§ 9-627. Determination of Commercially Reasonable Conduct

No preclusion of commercial reasonableness

The fact that a greater amount could have been obtained by a collection, enforcement, disposition, or acceptance at a different time or in a different method from that selected by the secured party is not sufficient to preclude the secured party from establishing that the collection, enforcement, disposition, or acceptance was commercially reasonable.

Commercially reasonable dispositions

Disposition of collateral is made in a commercially reasonable manner if:

1) in the usual manner on any recognized market;

2) at a price in a recognized market at the time of the disposition; or

3) otherwise in conformity with reasonable commercial practices among dealers in the type of property subject to disposition.

Approval by the court or on behalf of creditors

A collection, enforcement, disposition, or acceptance is commercially reasonable if it has been approved:

1) in a judicial proceeding;

2) by a *bona fide* creditors' committee;

3) by a representative of creditors; or

4) by an assignee for the benefit of creditors.

§ 9-628. Limitation on Liability for Secondary Obligor

Limitation of liability of a secured party for noncompliance

Unless a secured party knows that a person is a debtor or obligor, knows the identity of the person, and knows how to communicate with the person:

The secured party is not liable to the person, secured party, or lienholder that has filed a financing statement against the person for failure to comply with this article; and

The secured party's failure to comply with this article does not affect the liability of the person for a deficiency.

Limitation of liability based on status as a secured party

A secured party is not liable because of its status as a secured party:

1) to the debtor or obligor unless the secured party knows:

(A) that the person is a debtor or obligor;

(B) the identity of the person; and

(C) how to communicate with the person; or

2) to a secured party or lienholder that has filed a financing statement against a person unless the secured party knows:

(A) that the person is a debtor; and

(B) the identity of the person.

Limitation of liability in non-consumer-goods transactions

A secured party is not liable, and a person's liability for a deficiency is not affected because of an act or omission arising out of the secured party's reasonable belief that a transaction is not a consumer-goods transaction if the secured party's belief is based on reasonable reliance on:

1) a debtor's representation concerning the purpose for which collateral was to be used, acquired, or held; or

2) an obligor's representation concerning the purpose for which a secured obligation was incurred.

Limitation of multiple liabilities for statutory damages

A secured party is not liable more than once for one secured obligation.

Relationship matrix

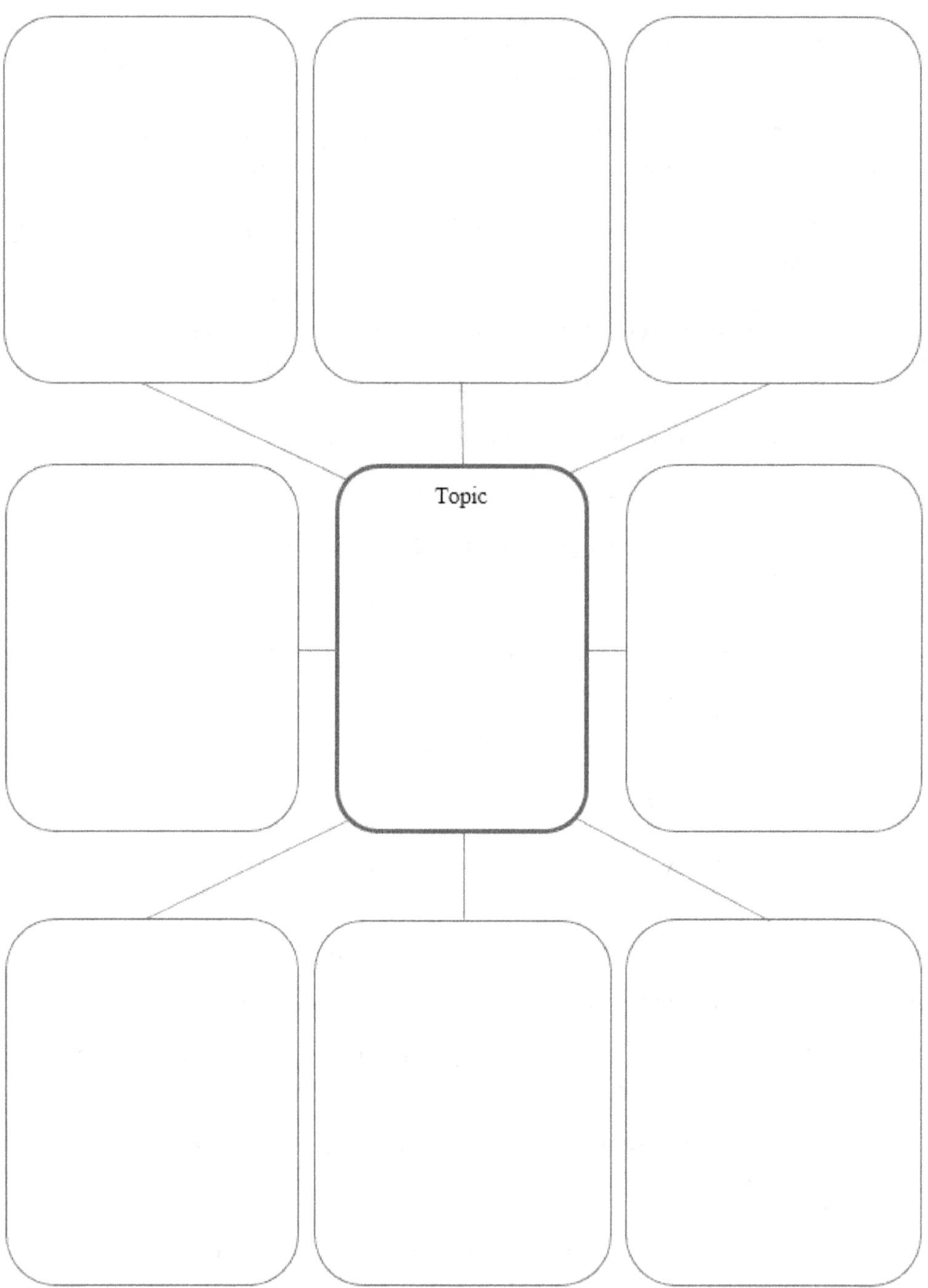

Notes for active learning

Notes for active learning

Bar Exam Information, Preparation
and
Test-Taking Strategies

Introduction to the Uniform Bar Examination (UBE)

Structure of the UBE

The Uniform Bar Examination (UBE) includes 1) the Multistate Bar Examination (MBE), 2) Multistate Essay Examination (MEE), and 3) Multistate Performance Test (MPT).

The MBE has 200 multiple-choice questions accounting for 50% of the UBE.

The MEE has six essays worth 30% of the UBE score.

The MPT has two legal tasks (e.g., complaint, client letter) for 20% of the UBE score.

The Multistate Bar Examination (MBE)

The Multistate Bar Examination consists of 200 four-option multiple-choice questions prepared by the National Conference of Bar Examiners (NCBE).

Of these 200 questions, 175 are scored, and 25 are unscored pretest questions.

Candidates answer 100 questions in the three-hour morning session and the remaining 100 questions in the three-hour afternoon session.

The 175 scored questions are distributed with 25 questions on each of the seven subject areas: Federal Civil Procedure, Constitutional Law, Contracts, Criminal Law and Procedure, Evidence, Real Property, and Torts.

A specified percentage of questions in each subject tests topics in those subjects.

For example, approximately one-third of Evidence questions test hearsay and its exceptions, while approximately one-third of Torts questions test negligence.

Interpreting the UBE score report

Overall score. The National Conference of Bar Examiners (NCBE) states the Uniform Bar Exam (UBE) requires a passing scaled score between 260 to 280. Scores above 280 receive a passing score in every UBE state.

The "percentile" is the number of people that scored lower. If an examinee scored in the 47th percentile, they scored higher than 47% of the examinees (and lower than 53%).

The examinee is first given a "raw score,"; based on the number of correct answers.

The raw score is adjusted by adding points to achieve the "scaled score." The number of points added is determined by a formula that compares the difficulty of the current exam to prior benchmark exams.

The comparative performance of examinees on "control questions" (prior pretest questions) given on previous exams form the basis for determining each exam's difficulty.

MBE scaled score. Examinees receive a scaled score and not an MBE "raw" score (i.e., the number of correct answers). MBE scores are scaled scores calculated by the NCBE through a statistical process used for standardized tests.

According to the NCBE, this statistical process adjusts raw scores on the current exam to account for differences in difficulty compared to previously administered exams. The scaled score is calculated from the raw score, but the NCBE does not publish the conversion formula.

Since the MBE is a scaled score, equating makes it impossible to know precisely how many questions must be answered correctly to receive a particular score. Equating allows scores from different exams to be compared since a specific scaled score represents the same level of knowledge among exams.

The MBE is curved, so just because a score is "close" to passing does not mean you are close. For example, a 124 may be in the 31st percentile and a 136 in the 62nd percentile. A 12-point difference in scaled scores equates to a 31-point percentile difference. If you are in the 120s, much preparation is needed to increase your score.

For most states, aim for a scaled score of 135 to "pass" the MBE. If you are unsure what score you need, divide the passing score by two. For example, if a 270 is needed to pass the bar, divide 268 by two to yield 135 as a threshold score on the MBE.

The importance of the MBE score

A passing MBE score depends on the jurisdiction. In jurisdictions that score on a 200-point scale, the passing score is the overall score. Passing scores are often approximately 135.

For the July 2020 bar exam, the national average MBE score was 146.1, an increase of 5 points from the July 2019 national average of 141.1.

For comparison, on the July 2018 bar, the national average MBE score was 139.5, a decrease of about 2.2 points from the July 2017 national average of 141.7.

How much the MBE contributes depends on the jurisdiction. Each jurisdiction has its policy for the relative weight given to the MBE compared to other bar exam components.

For Uniform Bar Examination (UBE) jurisdictions, the MBE component is 50%.

Most jurisdictions combine the MBE score with the state essay exam score.

The overall state candidates' performance on the MBE controls the raw state essay's conversion to scaled scores. Achieve a scaled MBE score of at least 135 to pass the bar.

MEE and MPT scores

In a UBE score report, there are six scores for the Multistate Essay Exam (MEE) and two for the Multistate Performance Test (MPT). Most states release this information.

Most states grade on a 1–6 scale (some use another scale).

In states grading on a 1–6 scale, 4 is considered a passing score.

The MEE and MPT sections are not weighted equally.

The MEE essays are worth 60%, while the MPT is 40% of the written score.

Many examinees assume that they passed the MPT and MEE portions of the exam. Examine the score report to see how you performed on these portions.

The objective of the Multistate Bar Exam

Working knowledge of the MBE objectives, the skills it tests, how it is drafted, the relationship of the parts of an MBE question, and the testing limitations provide you a substantial advantage in choosing the correct answers to MBE questions and passing the bar.

Knowing which issues are tested and the form in which they are tested makes it more manageable to learn the large body of substantive law.

The MBE's fundamental objective is to measure fairly, and efficiently which law school graduates have the necessary academic qualifications to be admitted to the bar and exceed this threshold.

The multiple-choice exam used to accomplish this objective must be of a consistent level of difficulty.

The level at which the pass decision is made must be achievable by most candidates.

The MBE tests the following skills:

- reading carefully and critically

- identifying the legal issue in a set of facts

- knowing the law that governs the legal issues tested

- distinguish between frequently confused closely-related principles

- making reasonable judgments from ambiguous facts

- understanding how limiting words make plausible-sounding choices wrong

- choosing the correct answer by intelligently eliminating incorrect choices

Preparation Strategies for the Bar Exam

An effective bar exam study plan

There are a lot of great ideas about how to prepare. Follow through with these ideas and turn them into persistent action for successful preparation.

A detailed and well-planned study schedule has benefits, such as giving you a sense of control and building confidence and proficiency.

Pick a date about 12-14 weeks before the exam (November for the February exam and April for the July exam) and use it as the start of your active study period.

Start a month earlier than many others to have a month to review as final preparation at the end.

Students have found this effective. Use an elongated prep period as a study schedule.

Most examinees prefer at least two weeks before the exam to review the material.

By planning early, you will have more time. You may want three or four final weeks to review subjects, take timed exams, and ensure that you are prepared to take the exam.

A few notes on schedule management:

> Do not *start* memorizing during your initial review period. You should be learning every week from the beginning of your study schedule. This final prep period is for reviewing and taking timed exams.

> If you stretch the study schedule over several months, plan review weeks into your schedule. For example, every four weeks, use a few days to review the governing law and take timed exams. This is a practical and fruitful approach as you will be more likely to retain the information.

Pick specific dates for specific tasks; this makes it more likely you will complete them.

Make sure the tasks are measurable. (e.g., practice two MEE essays).

Be realistic about the tasks, time, energy, and your ability to complete the items listed as tasks in preparation for the exam.

Remember to take some scheduled breaks from studying.

Exercise, sleep and take care of your physical and mental health.

If you are not in the right mental state preparing for the exam, you will likely be ineffective when studying and are less likely to pass the exam.

Focused studying

Some people are better at multiple-choice questions; others do better with essays.

The multiple-choice portion (MBE at 50%) and the essay portion (MEE at 30% and MPT at 20%) are weighted equally.

Doing poorly in one section means it will be challenging to achieve a passing score.

Identify weaknesses early in the preparation process and focus on them.

If you struggle with multiple-choice questions, dedicate extra time to practicing MBE questions.

If you struggle with writing, focus on completing MEE essays and complete MPT practice materials.

By reviewing your performance on released multiple-choice practice tests, be concerned if you consistently miss questions that are most answered correctly.

If you have problems with questions and perform below 50%, you lack the fundamental knowledge necessary to pass the MBE.

When reviewing your answers to practice questions, it is essential to review all questions and answers, even those you got right.

Make sure you got that correct answer for the right reason.

Reviewing the questions and answers is critical for success on the exam.

Spend time reviewing those basic principles and working deliberately on the straightforward (and easy) questions that supplement learning.

Advice on using outlines

As a user of this governing law book, several of the following points are moot. They are included, so you can be confident that you are using the proper resources to prep for the bar.

Having a useful governing law study guide (such as this book) is critical.

Without effective resources, it is challenging to understand, learn and apply the governing law to the facts given in the question.

Some students use outlines that make learning difficult.

A few common mistakes about outlines:

- Learning outlines that are too long (e.g., more than 100 pages per subject) or too short (e.g., a seven-page Contracts outline). You will be overwhelmed by information or never learn enough governing law.

- Spending too much time comparing several outlines for the same subject.

For example, using different Contracts outlines and needlessly comparing them. This confusion results in an undue focus on insignificant discrepancies.

- Outlining every subject. If you are not starting to study early, this consumes too much study time. Do not attempt to outline all subjects. It may be a good idea to outline a select few problematic subjects.

Using a detailed and well-organized governing law outline (e.g., this book) is essential; it saves time, organizes concepts, reduces anxiety, and helps you score well and pass the bar.

Easy questions make the difference

Limitations on the examiners lead to the first important insight into preparation for the exam – the kind of questions that decide whether you pass.

Performance on specific questions correlates with success or failure on the bar.

By analyzing statistics, questions predicting success or failure have been identified.

In general, the most challenging questions were not particularly good predictors of failure because most people who missed them passed the bar.

However, many of the straightforward questions were excellent predictors of success.

The median raw score ranges from about 60% to 66% correct on the MBE.

The National Conference of Bar Examiners (NCBE) writes, "expert panelists reported that they believed MBE items were generally easy, correctly estimating that about 66% of candidates would select the right answer to a typical item."

Depending on the exam's difficulty, in most states, scoring slightly below the median (miss up to 80 questions) still passes.

The most important questions to determine if you pass are not the exceedingly challenging ones but the easy ones where 90% of the examinees answer correctly.

The easy questions usually test a basic and regularly tested point of substantive law.

The wrong choices (i.e., the distracters) are typically easy to eliminate.

Your first task in preparing for the MBE is to get easy questions correct.

Study plan based upon statistics

These statistics show that an excellent performance on either the MBE questions (approximately 67% correct) or the state essays (4s on essays) assures you a passing score.

If you fail the MBE by 9 points or the essays by 5 points, the probability of passing the bar is in the single digits.

Put effort into performing well on the MBE questions for the following reasons.

- The questions are objective, and there are enough questions that are predictable concerning content and structure that it is possible, through reasonable effort, to answer 67% of the questions correctly.

- Studying the MBE first has the added advantage of preparing the necessary substantive law for state essays.

- The essays cover several subjects, the precise topic tested is unpredictable, and the answers are graded subjectively by graders who work quickly.

You had three years of law school practice with essays and less experience with multiple-choice questions.

Master the MBE before spending time preparing for the essays.

Factors associated with passing the bar

Based on an analysis of statistics from students' performance, the following factors predict the likelihood of passing the bar:

LSAT score

First-year Grade Point Average (GPA)

LSAT scores are a significant predictor of success on the bar because the LSAT requires similar multiple-choice test-taking skills as the MBE.

The LSAT tests many of the types of legal reasoning tested on the MBE.

A lower LSAT can be overcome by a comprehensive study of the MBE governing law, but these students must work harder.

Most of the subjects tested (e.g., constitutional law, civil procedure, contracts, criminal law, real property, torts) on the MBE are taken in the first year of law school.

First-year GPA measures mastery of subjects, preparedness for exams, and the ability to understand legal principles and apply them to given fact patterns.

The MBE measures the same factors but in a multiple-choice format instead of essays.

Pass rates based on GPA and LSAT scores

Past statistics indicate that law students with LSAT scores above 155 and a first-year GPA above 3.0 are reasonably assured of passing the bar.

They should study conscientiously and take practice MBEs to perform at the level needed, but they have little cause to panic.

Students with LSAT scores between 150 and 155 and a first-year GPA between 2.5 and 3.0 are in a bit more danger of failing and need to undertake rigorous preparation.

They must achieve a scaled score of 135 and take released practice exams and understand the reasons for incorrect choices. They should prepare for state essays by learning the governing laws in this book.

Students with LSAT scores between 145 and 150 and a first-year GPA between 2.2 and 2.5 have a moderate chance of passing the bar from deliberate efforts.

These students should not rely on ordinary commercial bar reviews and need intense training, particularly on the MBE component of the bar. They must devote 50-60 hours per week for seven weeks to prepare for the bar by learning the format and content of substantive law tested on the MBE. They should take released practice exams under exam conditions and conscientiously study the questions missed.

Students with LSAT scores below 145 and a GPA below 2.2 have had a failure rate of approximately 80%.

They must prep faithfully and conscientiously beyond the advice above and must engage in a rigorous course of study, more than is demanded by a traditional bar review course.

Learning and Applying the Substantive Law

Knowledge of substantive law

The fundamental reason for missing a question is 1) a failure to know the principle of law controlling the answer or 2) failure to understand how that principle is applied.

You must know and apply the governing law to pass the bar. If you do not know the governing law, you will not apply it to answer correctly.

Many students *think* they understand the governing law but do not know the nuances. Do not assume that you understand the governing (i.e., substantive) law. It is prevalent for students not to know the governing law well.

Re-learn the substantive and procedural law taught in first-year courses.

A major mistake is not to memorize the governing law outlined in this book.

The multiple-choice and essay portions test nuances and details of governing law. It is essential to analyze the governing law as it is applied in the context of the question.

On the multiple-choice section, many questions require fine-line distinctions between similar principles of law.

Several multiple-choice answers will *seem* correct, given the limited time to answer. If your knowledge of the governing law is suboptimal, you will not make these subtle distinctions and will have to guess on many questions.

For the essay to be developed, you must know the governing law and apply it to the issues within the call of the question.

If you do not know the governing law, you will not state the correct rule in your essay. You will be unable to apply the correct rule to the fact pattern.

Where to find the law

The questions must be related to the subject matter outlined in the bar examiners' (NCBE) materials.

While the NCBE outline is broad and ambiguous, years of experience with the exam delineate the scope of material you must learn.

The governing law covered in this book is foundational to the exam. The governing law statements were compiled by analyzing questions released by the multistate examiners. The analysis revealed a limited number of legal principles repeatedly tested.

Review these principles before taking practice exams and understand how they are applied to obtain the correct answer.

The property questions are probably the most difficult. The fact patterns are usually long and involve many parties in complex transactions.

In preparing for the exam, learn basic property principles and apply them. However, extensive studying into property law's crevices is not necessary to score well on these questions.

Feel confident that you do not have to go beyond the information provided in this book to find the governing law.

Controlling authority

The examiners have specified the sources of authority for the correct answers.

In Constitutional Law and Criminal Procedure, it is Supreme Court decisions.

In Criminal Law, it is common law.

In Evidence, the Federal Rules of Evidence controls.

In Torts and Property, it is the generally accepted view of United States law.

The UCC is the controlling authority in sales (Article 2) questions.

The NCBE released questions, and the published answers determine the controlling law through deduction.

Recent changes in the law

The exam is prepared months before it is given because of logistical requirements. Therefore, the examiners cannot incorporate recent changes in the law into the questions.

Recent changes in the law will not form the basis for correct answers.

If a recent change makes an answer initially designated as the correct answer to be incorrect, the examiners will credit more than one answer.

The recent holding of a Supreme Court case will not be tested for about two years since the decision was published.

Lesser-known issues and unusual applications

Some of the challenging exam questions are based on obscure principles of law.

Missing the most challenging questions will not cause you to fail the exam if you have a solid understanding of the governing law. You can learn these principles and answer the question correctly, thereby improving your overall performance.

There are instances where the correct answers are different from the usual rules.

For example, hearsay evidence inadmissible at trial is admissible before a judge hearing evidence on a preliminary question of fact (e.g., Federal Rules of Evidence 104(a)).

Practice applying the governing law

Some students know the governing law but have problems *applying* it to the facts.

The exam is as much about testing skills as it is about testing the governing law.

Therefore, knowledge of the governing law is not enough to pass.

You must practice answering multiple-choice questions and writing well-organized, coherent, and complete essays where you apply the governing law to the given facts.

Know which governing law is being tested

A typical wrong answer (i.e., distracter) on a question is an answer which is correct under a body of law other than the governing law being tested.

An example is a question governed by Article 2 of the Uniform Commercial Code (UCC), where an offer is irrevocable if:

1) it is in writing,

2) made by a merchant, and

3) states that it is irrevocable.

One of the wrong answers states the correct rule under the common law of contracts, where an offer is revocable unless consideration is paid (i.e., an option) for the promise to keep it open.

Answers which are always wrong

Some commonly used distracters are always wrong and can be eliminated quickly.

For example, a choice in an evidence question says, "character can only be attacked by reputation evidence." This choice is wrong because both opinion and reputation evidence is admissible under the Federal Rules of Evidence when character attacks are permissible.

Honing Reading Skills

Reading skills are critical. The basic level is reading to understand the facts, identify the issue and keep the parties distinct. A mistake at this juncture results in answering incorrectly, no matter how much law is known.

Understanding complex transactions

If the question involves a transaction with many parties, diagram the transaction before analyzing the choices.

The diagram should show the relationship between the parties (e.g., grantor-grantee, assignor-assignee), the transaction date, and the person's relationships in the transaction (e.g., donee, *bona fide* purchaser).

Impediments to careful reading

Two reasons candidates fail to read carefully are:

1)   hurrying through a question,

2)   fatigue due to a lack of sleep or strain caused by the exam.

A careful test taker maintains a steady, deliberate pace during the exam. Practice in advance and be well-rested on the test day.

Reading too much into a question

The examiners are committed to designing questions, which are "a fair index of whether the applicant has the ability to practice law." Psychometric experts ensure that they are fair and unbiased.

Even though you must read every word of these carefully drafted questions, do not read the question to find some bizarre interpretation.

The examiners must ask fair questions and not rely on "tricks." Reading too much into a question and looking for a trick lurking behind every fact leads to the wrong answer often.

It is the straightforward questions that determine whether you pass, not the occasional challenging question that tests some arcane principle of law.

Therefore, take questions at face value.

Read the call of the question first

Before reading the facts, read the call of the question because it indicates the task for selecting the correct answer. This perspective focuses your attention before reading the facts.

The question contains many *words of art*, such as "most likely," "best defense," or "least likely," which govern the correct answer.

The call is often phrased positively; the "best argument" or "most likely result."

Read answers for consistency with the question and eliminate inconsistent choices.

Negative calls

When the call of the question is negative, asking for the "weakest argument" or asking which of the options is "not" in a specified category, examine each option with the perspective that the choice with those negative characteristics is the correct answer.

After reading and understanding the question stem, read the call of the question again before reading the choices.

Analyze each choice with the requirements specified in the call of the question.

Read all choices

Never pick an answer until carefully reading all the choices. The objective is to pick the best answer, which cannot be determined until comparing the choices.

Sometimes the difference between the right and wrong answer is that one choice is more detailed or precisely sets forth the applicable law. You do not know that until reading all the answers carefully.

Broad statements of black letter law may be correct

When reading an answer, do not rule out choices with imprecise statements of the applicable *black letter* law.

If the examiners always included a choice that was precisely on point, the questions would be too easy. Instead, they often disguise the wording used in the correct answer.

For example, the Federal Rules of Evidence contain an elaborate set of relevancy rules that limit the right to introduce evidence of repairs after an accident. If there was a question where the introduction of that evidence was permissible, and no choices specifically cite the exception to the general rule of exclusion, an answer phrased with the general rule of relevancy "Admissible because its probative value outweighs its prejudicial effect," would be the correct answer.

Multiple-Choice Test-Taking Tactics

Determine the single correct answer

Increase the odds of picking the correct answer based on technical factors independent of substantive (governing) law knowledge.

The examiners' limitation is that every question must have one demonstrably correct and three demonstrably incorrect answers, limiting how the examiners write the choices.

From the question's construction, this limitation may give clues about the answer.

Process of elimination

Answering a multiple-choice question is not finding the ideal answer to the question asked but instead picking the best option.

Eliminate choices and evaluate the remaining choice for plausibility.

Eliminate choices that state an incorrect proposition of law or do not relate to the facts.

If you eliminate three options and the remaining one is acceptable, pick it and move on.

Elimination increases the odds

It takes about 125 correct answers to pass the MBE. An important strategy in reaching that number is intelligently eliminating choices.

If you are sure of the answer to only 50 of the 200 questions on the exam and confidently eliminate two of the four choices on the remaining 150 questions. Guess between the two remaining choices, and the odds predict 75 correct.

Those 75 correct, coupled with 50 questions you were confident of the answer, produce a raw score of 125 on the MBE and a scaled score above the benchmark 135.

Unfortunately, you cannot avoid guessing on questions, but intelligent methods reduce options to only two viable choices.

Sometimes you might not be able to eliminate the wrong answers just because you are sure of the answer to one of the choices. Eliminating with confidence even one choice increases the probability of correctly answering the question.

Eliminating two wrong answers

Specific questions on the MBE are challenging because of distinguishing between two choices when selecting the best answer.

A typical comment from examinees leaving the exam is, "I could not decide between the last two choices."

The positive side of that problem is eliminating two of the four choices.

Pick the winning side

The most common choice pattern is the "two-two" pattern – two choices state that the plaintiff prevails, and two that the defendant prevails.

The best approach for this type of question is to rely on your knowledge of the law or instinctive feeling to which conclusion is correct.

In a question with two choices on one side and two on the other side of a court's decision, first, pick a choice on the side you think should prevail.

Distinguish between the explanations following this conclusion and pick the choice that best justifies it.

Distance between choices on the other side

If the justifications following the conclusion for the side you chose seem indistinguishable, look at the explanations for the choices on the other side.

If the reasons for the choices on the other side are readily distinguishable, and one appears reasonable and the other incorrect, reconsider your initial conclusion.

Remember, the examiner is required to provide a distinguishable reason why one explanation of a general conclusion is correct, and the other is wrong.

That obligation does not exist if the general conclusion itself is incorrect.

Suppose choices (A) and (B) on one side look correct; that is, they are reasonable and consistent with the fact pattern. One of the choices with the opposite conclusion, answer (C), seems incorrect or inconsistent with the facts, and answer (D) with the same general conclusion sounds reasonable. From a strictly technical viewpoint, the best choice is answer (D).

Questions based upon a common fact pattern

There are several instances where two or more questions are based on the same facts.

Look at the second question's wording to guide the first question's correct answer. When asked to assume an answer to a first question from a fact pattern to answer the second question, the probability is high that the answer to the first question follows that assumption.

For example, if the first question has two choices beginning with "P prevails" and two with "D prevails," and the second question starts with "If P prevails," it is likely one of the "P prevails" choices is correct for the first question. If you picked "D prevails," think carefully before selecting it as the final answer.

Multiple true/false issues

In addition to true/false questions, the exam sometimes states three propositions in the root of the question and tests characteristics of those propositions in the call of the question.

The choices list various combinations of propositions.

The difference between this type of question and the double true/false question is that only four of the eight possible combinations fit into the options. It is possible to answer correctly even if you are not sure of all propositions' truth or falsity but are sure of one.

Correctly stated, but the inapplicable principle of law

The task of the examiners is to make the wrong choices look attractive. A creative way to accomplish this is to write a choice that impeccably states a rule of law that is not applicable because of facts in the root of the question.

For example, in a question where a person is an assignee, not a sublessee, one of the choices may correctly state the law for sublessees, but it is inapplicable to the fact pattern.

Therefore, these answer choices with inapplicable law can be confidently eliminated.

"Because" questions

Conjunctions are commonly used in the answers. It is essential to understand their role in determining whether a choice is correct.

The word "because" connects a conclusion and the reason for that conclusion with the facts in the body of the question.

There are two requirements for a question using "because" to be correct:

1) the conclusion must be correct,

2) the reasoning must logically follow based upon facts in the question, and the statement which follows "because" must be legally correct.

If the "because" choice has the correct result for the wrong reason, it is incorrect.

"If" questions

The conjunction "if" requires a much narrower focus than "because."

When a choice contains an "if," determine whether the entire statement is true, assuming that the proposition which follows the "if" is true.

There is no requirement that facts in the root of the question support the proposition following "if." There is no requirement for facts in the question to support the proposition that such a construction be reasonable.

"Because" or "if" need not be exclusive

There is no requirement for the conclusion following "if" or "because" to be exclusive.

For example, if a master could be liable in tort under the doctrine of *respondeat superior* or because the master was *negligent*, a choice using "if" or "because" holding the master liable would be correct if it stated either reason, even though the master might be liable for the other reason.

Exam tip for "because"

Notice that in an answer that would have been correct, the word "because" limits the facts you could consider to those in the body of the question containing specific facts.

The difference between the effect of "if" and "because" controls the answer.

Identify those limited situations (e.g., where the appropriate standard is strict liability) and distinguish them from those that are satisfactory (e.g., if the standard is negligence).

"Only if" requires exclusivity

Sometimes the words "only if" are used to distinguish between the two "affirmed" choices to make one wrong.

When an option uses the words "only if," assume that the entire proposition is correct as long as the words following "only if" are true.

The critical difference, where "only if" is used, is that the proposition cannot be true except when the condition is true. If there is another reason for the same result to be reached, the choice is wrong.

"Unless" questions

The conjunction "unless" has the same function as "only if," except that it precedes a negative exclusive condition instead of a positive exclusive condition.

It is essentially the mirror image of an "only if" choice.

For an option using "unless," reverse and substitute the words "only if" for "unless."

Limiting words

Choices can be made incorrect with limiting words that require that a proposition be true in all circumstances or under no circumstances.

Examples of limiting words include *all*, *any*, *never*, *always*, *only*, *every*, and *plenary*.

Making Correct Judgment Calls

Applying the law to the facts

Most questions give a fact pattern and ask which choice draws the correct legal conclusion required by the call of the question.

The first skill required is to draw inferences from facts given to place the conduct described in the question in the appropriate legal category.

The second skill is to apply the appropriate legal rule to conduct in that category and choose the option which reaches the appropriate conclusion.

The process of drawing inferences from a fact pattern and placing conduct in an appropriate category often requires judgment.

Bad judgment equals the wrong answer

To make the questions difficult, the examiners often place the conduct near the border of two different legal classifications.

Decide which side of the demarcation the conduct falls on. Inevitably, reasonable people can differ on these judgments.

If your judgment does not match the examiners, you will likely answer the question incorrectly, no matter how much law you know.

Mitigate this problem by reviewing released questions involving judgment calls where the examiners have published correct answers (i.e., their judgment call).

For example, a death occurring because the parties played Russian roulette is considered *depraved heart murder*, not *involuntary manslaughter*.

Judgment calls happen

Difficult judgment calls occur several times on the exam, and you are likely to make some close judgment calls incorrectly.

While this adds to the frustrations of multiple-choice tests, it is part of the exam.

By narrowing judgment call questions to two choices and guessing, you will get approximately half of them correct.

You will not fail the exam solely because you were unlucky on judgment calls.

The examiners remove many judgment calls by procedural devices.

The importance of procedure

The question may not ask what a jury should find on the facts.

The answer may be controlled by the procedural context of the criminal prosecution.

For example, it is given that the jury has found the defendant guilty of murder, and the only question on appeal is whether the judge should have granted a motion to dismiss at the end of hearing evidence. This is because a reasonable jury looking at the facts and inferences most favorable to the prosecution should not have found the defendant guilty of murder.

The same procedural issues exist when the question asks if a motion for summary judgment should be allowed or if the court should direct a verdict.

Exam Tips and Suggestions

Timing is everything

The time given to complete the exam is usually adequate if you practiced enough questions to improve speed and efficiency to the required level.

As you get closer to the test date, just doing practice questions is not enough.

You need to time your practice. Take previously released exams in two three-hour periods on the same day. Since these practice exams are approximately the same length as the exam, you will know if you have a timing problem.

If you do not practice under timed conditions, you risk exhausting time on the exam before answering all the questions.

Practice your timing under test-like conditions to know if the timing will be an issue. If you cannot complete the practice exam, you will have trouble with the exam.

If time is an issue, adjust your pace and continue practicing.

All questions do not require the same amount of time.

An approach for when time is not an issue

If you can complete 100 questions in three hours, use this strategy. At the start of the exam, break the allotted time into 15-minute intervals and write them down.

Set an initial pace of 9 questions every fifteen minutes.

Check your progress at each 15-minute interval.

If you completed 18 questions in the first half-hour, 36 in the first hour, 72 in the first two hours, and 90 in the first two and a half hours, you are on target to complete the exam on time. At this pace, you should complete 100 questions in two hours and forty-six minutes.

This leaves 14 minutes to check the answer sheet, revisit troublesome questions, or use the time to go a little slower on the last questions when fatigue impairs acuity.

If you find that your careful pace is faster than the budgeted 9 questions every 15 minutes, work at a faster pace, but use the extra time on the more challenging questions or in rechecking your work at the end.

Do *not* change the original answer choice unless you have a specific reason.

It is unwise to leave the exam early.

An approach for when time is an issue

During practice, continue answering questions to complete the section even after the time for self-paced exams has expired. Note which question you completed within the allocated time. Strive to complete the questions within the allotted time during your final exam prep.

If you learn from taking the practice test that you may not finish the questions in the allotted time on the actual exam, skip those questions with a long fact pattern followed by only one question. Keep your place on the answer sheet by skipping the row.

Return to those questions at the end and complete as many as time permits. Before turning your exam in, guess at the rest to reduce the number of random guesses.

Answer every question, even if you have not read the question, since wrong answers do *not* count against you.

Difficult questions

If you do not know the answer, do not spend a disproportionate amount of time on it since each question counts the same. Mark it in the test booklet, make a shrewd guess within the budgeted time and come back if time allows.

Do *not* leave questions unanswered. No points are deducted for wrong answers.

Minimize fatigue to maximize your score

The mental energy required to answer all the multiple-choice questions under stress produces fatigue (even with a lunch break).

Fatigue slows processing questions effectively and impairs reading comprehension. You may process questions more slowly at the end of each session and more quickly at the beginning before fatigue sets in.

Take at least two released exams under timed conditions to know how significantly fatigue affects your performance.

Be sure to arrive at the exam site on time. If necessary, stay at a nearby hotel rather than getting up early and risking a long drive the morning of the exam.

Relax during the lunch break and do not discuss the morning session with others.

You should know enough about your metabolism to eat the correct foods during the exam and reinforce appropriate caffeine levels if appropriate.

Proofread the answer sheet

As you decide on each correct answer, circle the corresponding letter in the exam book, and mark the appropriate block on the answer sheet.

The answer sheet is the only document graded by the examiners.

At the pace of 9 questions per 15 minutes, about 14 minutes should remain. Spend that time proofreading the answer sheet. Verify the answers circled to be certain that you marked the appropriate block on the answers.

Ensure that there are no blanks, and no questions have two answers.

Do *not* use this time to change an answer already selected unless you have a particularly good reason to change it.

If you have erased, ensure the erasure is thorough, or the computer may reject the answer because it cannot distinguish between marked answers.

If you have time after proofreading, review the problematic questions, and re-think the answers chosen. However, even after careful thought, hesitate to change an answer.

Do not leave any section of the exam early; use the allotted time wisely.

Intelligent preparation over a sustained period

There is no easy way to conquer an exam as challenging and comprehensive as the MBE, except through practice and an investment of time and effort well before the exam.

By diligently preparing, practicing questions, and intelligently assessing why questions were answered incorrectly, your skills for the exam will improve substantially.

Continue to improve those skills by following the advice given herein until reaching a proficiency level enabling you to pass the bar. This proficiency is accurately measured in multiple-choice format questions.

Some students will have to work harder to achieve the required proficiency.

The tools are in this study guide, and any law school graduate can be successful in passing the bar if they invest the required time and effort to be prepared.

Essay Preparation Strategies and Essay-Writing Suggestions

Memorize the law

Do not make the mistake of waiting too long before memorizing the governing law. Start learning the governing law early to be better prepared and pass the exam.

Memorize essential principles and focus on highly tested governing law.

Focus on the highly tested essay rules

Do not treat all subjects the same when you prepare for the essay portion of the exam.

Some governing law topics are tested more than others. It is crucial to focus on the highly tested topics (e.g., torts, contracts. property, civil procedure).

Know and apply enough governing laws to pass the bar – focus on commonly tested governing laws (e.g., negligence) provided in this book.

Practice writing essay answers each week

Practicing is crucial to a high score on essays. Practice regularly and avoid procrastination for this essential component of bar prep.

Incorporate practicing essay writing into your exam study schedule. To reduce procrastination, schedule time for writing practice essays each week.

For the MPT, practice by drafting full MPTs. Most examinees procrastinate on preparing for the MPT; there is nothing to memorize.

Do not make the *fatal mistake* of not practicing. The MPT portion is worth 20% of the UBE score.

Know the format and *practice that format to* increase your UBE score. This practice will increase your score and the probability of passing the bar.

Add one essay-specific subject each week

The Multistate Essay Exam (MEE) subjects include the 7 MBE subjects plus the 5 subjects of Business Associations (Agency, Partnerships, Corporations, and LLCs), Conflict of Laws, Family Law, Trusts and Estates, and Secured Transactions (UCC Article 9).

Combine highly tested subjects (e.g., torts) with less-tested subjects (e.g., secured transactions) and complex topics (e.g., contracts) with easier topics (e.g., business associations).

From preparation, know which subjects you struggle with and require a focused effort to master the essential governing law.

Make it easy for the grader to award points

Your answer to a question will probably be read in less than five minutes by a grader with a checklist to find that you have seen the issues and discussed them intelligently. Writing organized and clear answers makes it easy for the essay grader to award points.

Use headings for each of the major issues.

If the question suggests a structure for the answer because it is divided into parts or because the facts present a series of discrete issues, use the structure of the question, which is probably the structure of the checklist.

Use the IRAC method for the essay questions: state the issue, state the Rule. Apply the rule to the facts and conclude. IRAC seems simple, but following this approach makes it easier for the grader to know that you identified and addressed every issue and applied the law to the facts given.

IRAC results in more points during the exam.

Do not spend time trying to formulate eloquent issue statements. The question often outlines the issues, so an eloquent issue statement is redundant, and issue statements do not earn extra points.

Many examinees spend too much time developing an impressive issue statement and omit other essentials of their analysis (e.g., truncated analysis section).

An issue statement "Torts" or "Is the defendant liable for negligence?" is enough.

Do not waste time arguing both sides. There are no "two sides" for many essays to argue on bar essays because these are not law school essays.

Apply the law to facts and conclude unless asserting each party has good arguments.

Conclusion for each essay question

Points will be lost unless you conclude for each issue identified in the facts or are asked to address it in the call of the question.

Use caution starting the essay with the conclusion unless confident it is correct.

Many sample answers provided by the National Conference of Bar Examiners start with a definite and strong conclusion. Use caution to start with a conclusion unless confident (e.g., NCBE sample responses) your conclusion is correct.

Starting with a conclusion that is not correct draws attention to an incorrect conclusion at the start, which may influence the grader disproportionality. The grader may lose faith in your answer from the onset, and it is advisable to have a neutral heading rather than a firm conclusion that is wrong.

Tips for an easy-to-read essay

Use paragraph breaks between the Issue, Rule, Analysis, and Conclusion. Paragraph break makes it easy for the grader to read and score your essays. Additionally, this approach makes the answer appear longer and more complete.

Emphasize keywords and phrases. Underline key phrases so the grader notices that you addressed the governing law and applied it to the facts given.

After graders score several essays on the same topic, they scan essays for specific phrases that they expect to locate within a complete essay.

Think before you write

Read each question carefully to understand the facts and their necessary implications thoroughly and accurately.

After skimming the question, spend time on the focus line at the end of the question. Review the facts with the call of the question in mental focus.

Write a short outline of the issues raised. Outline in your mind the issues; state to yourself the tentative conclusions; test each conclusion from the standpoints of law and common sense; revise, as necessary.

Decide on a logical, orderly, and convincing arrangement for the response. Until then, you are not ready to write the answer.

Of the thirty-six minutes allotted to each essay, spend 15 minutes on issue spotting and organization and about twenty minutes writing the answer.

The ability to think and communicate like a lawyer

The Board knows that you have completed law school, under competent instructors, and have passed law school exams. The bar does not challenge the results of your law school courses.

The exam tests the ability to apply what you have learned to facts that might arise in practice and which, in some instances, involve several fields of law. The value of an answer depends not only on the correctness of the conclusions but on displaying essential legal principles and thinking like a lawyer.

Conclude on each issue presented. If a conclusion is derived from fuzzy facts, construct a well-reasoned argument supporting your conclusion to receive full credit regardless of if you conclude the same as the examiners.

If the correct answer depends on a provision of substantive law, which you are not familiar with, you can obtain a passing answer to the question by reaching a well-reasoned conclusion applying general law principles.

Do not try to limit the question to a particular subject area. Many questions combine traditional subjects, and you must be prepared to answer the question applying principles you learned across various subjects.

Do not restate the facts

The examiners know the facts; there is no time to waste. Do not restate the facts but use them to apply and integrate legal principles in writing the essay.

Do not fight the facts, particularly the focus line of the question.

For example, if the facts state that A executed a valid will, write about valid wills. If the question asks you to argue on behalf of A, do not argue on behalf of B because B has a prevailing argument. However, raise potential arguments which could be made on behalf of B and counter them in arguing on behalf of A.

Do not state abstract or irrelevant propositions of law

It is usually undesirable to begin an answer with a legal proposition. If the proposition is applicable, it will be more appropriate later to indicate the reason for your conclusion. If it is not applicable, do not state a surplus fact or legal principle.

Although it is seldom necessary to state an applicable rule of law in detail, make a sufficient reference to it so that the examiner appreciates your knowledge of the principle and conditions when it applies.

Do not, by speculating on different facts, nor in other ways, work into your answer some point of law with which you happen to be familiar, but which does not apply to the answer. Importantly, the examiners are not interested in knowing how many rules of law you know, but your ability to apply the applicable rules to the facts.

If the question says that A and B in the above hypothetical are unrelated, do not talk about the results which would occur if they were husband and wife.

Use the principles of law applicable to the call of the question and the facts. You must state the principles of applicable law to demonstrate to the examiner that you know the elements of the rule and how they apply to these facts.

For example, if the facts said that A transferred to B (a non-relative) the money necessary for B to purchase Blackacre from C and asks who owns Blackacre, you would say, "Since A furnished the consideration for the purchase of Blackacre and B took the title to the property in their name, B holds title to Blackacre in a resulting trust for A.

Do not detail the black letter law of resulting trusts since you have shown your knowledge by properly applying the facts to the law of resulting trusts.

Do not fight the facts and address a contrary fact not presented. The examiners may take points away if you make that mistake because you are not focused on the issues presented.

Discuss all the issues raised

A grasp of all the issues is essential.

For example, if there are three issues in a question, a discussion of only one issue, no matter how masterly, if coupled with omitting the others, could not result in 100% credit. It would probably result in a score of 33%.

The exam includes many issues in most questions so it can be graded mechanically. This maintains consistency across a group of several graders for each exam question.

The grader has a checklist of issues and awards most points for the examinee that identifies issues and intelligently discusses each.

Failure to see and discuss enough issues intelligently is probably the biggest reason for failure on the essay portion of the exam.

Methods for finding all issues

Use all the facts presented. Failure to discuss facts probably means that you missed important issues.

If you must decide in the early part of the question (e.g., does the court have jurisdiction) and you decide that issue so the remaining facts become irrelevant, make an alternative assumption ("If the court does have jurisdiction") and answer the question in the alternative using facts which would otherwise be irrelevant.

Do not avoid issues because you are not sure of the substantive law. If the examiners stated that X's nephew helped X escape after a crime, discuss the nephew's status as an accessory after the fact. If you do not know whether he is a close enough relative to be exempt under the statute, answer this issue by making alternative assumptions.

Indicators requiring alternative arguments

Ambiguous terms – if there are words in the fact pattern that are neutral or ambiguous such as "put up," the examiners look for possible interpretations of these terms.

Language in quotes – language placed in quotes is almost always ambiguous and must be construed as part of the answer.

Avoid ambiguous, rambling statements and verbosity

Generally, do not use compound sentences. Two separate sentences are preferred.

Complex sentences are particularly useful to apply the facts of the question to the applicable principle of law.

For example, in the previous resulting trust hypothetical, write, "Since B purchased Blackacre and took title in their name with money furnished by A, A holds title to Blackacre in a resulting trust, even if B has not signed a memorandum."

Avoid undue repetition

If the same principle of law and conclusion apply to two parts of an answer, state it once in detail, and refer back for the second part.

For example, if you have discussed A's liability and now must discuss B's liability, say, "B is also guilty of murder for the same reasons as A. (see discussion above)."

Avoid slang and colloquialism

The examiners judge your formal writing style.

If the examiner shows humor with names and events, do not show your sense of humor.

Use the standard abbreviations:

P for Plaintiff

D for Defendant

K for Contract

BFP for *Bona Fide* purchaser

Write legibly and coherently

Printing is usually easier to read than handwriting.

Use all the pages, and do not crowd your answer.

Plan your answer so that you do not have to use inserts and arrows.

Timing strategies

On the MEE, you must complete six equally weighted essay questions in three hours; an average of 30 minutes per question.

You have flexibility with time limitations as questions are not of the same difficulty.

There are two absolute figures:

spend no more than 45 minutes on any question,

spend at least 20 minutes on each question.

Be careful about not going over the time limit on the first question because this will require a readjustment of your timing for the entire session. If you miss the deadlines, re-divide your remaining time so that you will have an equal amount of time on each question.

If you go over by 15 minutes a question, do not allocate 30 minutes for other questions.

Stay focused

Do not start by reading the entire exam. Answer the questions in order and do not consider more than one question at a time.

After answering, put it out of your mind and not worry about your response. Keep your mind clear to focus on the next question.

Proofread your answers as time permits.

Best wishes with your preparation!

Law Essentials series

Constitutional Law	Criminal Law and Criminal Procedure
Contracts	Business Associations
Evidence	Conflict of Laws
Real Property	Family Law
Torts	Secured Transactions
Civil Procedure	Trusts and Estates

Visit our Amazon store

Comprehensive Glossary of Legal Terms

Over 2,100 essential legal terms defined
and explained. An excellent reference
source for law students, practitioners and
readers seeking an understanding of legal
vocabulary and its application.

Landmark U.S. Supreme Court Cases:
Essential Summaries

Learn important constitutional cases that
shaped American law. Understand how the
evolving needs of society intersect with the
U.S. Constitution. Short summaries of seminal
Supreme Court cases focused on issues and
holdings.

Visit our Amazon store

　Copyright © 2022 Sterling Test Prep.

Frank J. Addivinola, Ph.D., J.D., L.LM., MBA

The lead author and chief editor of this preparation guide is Dr. Frank Addivinola. With his outstanding education, professional training, legal and business experience, and university teaching, Dr. Addivinola lent his expertise to develop this book.

Attorney Frank Addivinola is admitted to practice law in several jurisdictions. He has served as an academic advisor and mentor for students and practitioners.

Dr. Addivinola holds an undergraduate degree from Williams College. He completed his Masters at Harvard University, Masters in Biotechnology at Johns Hopkins University, Masters in Technology Management and MBA at the University of Maryland University College, J.D. and L.LM. from Suffolk University, and Ph.D. in Law and Public Policy from Northeastern University.

During his extensive teaching career, Dr. Addivinola taught university courses in Introduction to Law and developed law coursebooks. He received several awards for community service, research, and presentations.